The
MOUNT
WASHINGTON
COG
RAILWAY

Climbing the White Mountains
of New Hampshire

BRUCE D. HEALD

THE
History
PRESS

Published by The History Press
Charleston, SC 29403
www.historypress.net

First published 2011

ISBN 978.1.60949.196.3

Library of Congress Cataloging-in-Publication Data

Heald, Bruce D., 1935-
The Mount Washington Cog Railway : climbing the White Mountains of New Hampshire
/ Bruce D. Heald.
p. cm.
Includes bibliographical references and index.
ISBN 978-1-54020-566-7
1. Mount Washington Cog Railway. 2. White Mountains (N.H. and Me.) I. Title.
TF688.M685H43 2011
385'.6--dc22
2011000880

For all the visitors to New Hampshire who enjoy celebrating the White Mountains via the Mount Washington Cog Railway.

Contents

The Mount Washington Cog Railway locomotive ascends Mount Washington.

Introduction

Superlatives can hardly render the magnificent views from the Presidential Range in the White Mountains. The romance of the ascent of Mount Washington—via the Cog Railway, the Auto Road or even hiking the wooded trails—is an adventure. Every mile of approach opens a new series of prospects, each of which has its own particular attraction and reveals the natural grandeur of its landscape. The different formations of the mountain ranges also call forth admiration of their scenic beauty—the brilliance of the Presidential Range contrasted with the southern wilderness of the Sandwich Range.

It was Sylvester Marsh who had a dream of ascending Mount Washington by rail, a dream many thought impossible. For Mr. Marsh, impossible was not in his vocabulary. So he set forth to fulfill his quest: to build his "Cog" Railway up the mountain so tourists could enjoy the splendor of scenery from his railway and from the summit of Mount Washington.

During the 1850s, Sylvester Marsh, a retired businessman, proposed to build a railroad to the summit of Mount Washington. When the legislature granted him a charter, it included permission to build a railroad to the top of Mount Lafayette. A waggish solon proposed that he should also be given permission to build a railroad to the moon. The charter was granted in 1858, and work began eight years later. With the aid of Walter Aiken, who designed the cogwheel engine, a quarter mile of track was completed for a demonstration. This convinced the Boston, Concord & Montreal Railroad officials of the practicability of the scheme, and Marsh secured their financial assistance.

The process of building was very slow and required three years to complete. The entire stretch of three and a third miles was opened to the public on July 3, 1869, and has been in constant operation during the summer months ever since.

When the first season opened, it was Old Peppersass that left the base station for the ascent of the mountain. Old Peppersass was the first locomotive to ever climb the mountain. The odd little train of one car, pushed by an ungainly but powerful engine, began its ascent by a grade of one foot in three through a broad and straight clearing in the woods. Ahead were the towering shoulders of Mount Washington, while behind, through the opening panorama, was the western group of mountains. Gradually, the trees on either side began to thin out and become smaller until they no longer obscured the views north and south. Shortly, Jacob's Ladder, a long and massive trestle, was reached, and here the steepest grade of the trip was encountered. The tree line was passed, and the locomotive entered the region of subalpine vegetation.

Fantastic views opened on all sides of the rocky humps of Mount Clay, drawing near to the site of the Great Gulf tank. Soon, an awe-inspiring view of the bowl-shaped Great Gulf itself appeared, and beyond, Mount Washington's nearest rival. The remainder of the trip was across a wide and comparatively flat area of gray and frost-splintered rocks with dull mosses and alpine flowers. The most magnificent display of color occurs when the early frost of autumn and the full ripening of leaves combine to produce a matchless pageantry of gold and scarlet, causing the spectacular vista on which the highlands are arrayed.

Reminisce for a moment about when the railroad was king of transportation during the late 1800s and the Boston, Concord & Montreal Railroad commanded the North Country. Later came the Boston & Maine Railroad, which traveled up the stately, pastoral Pemigewasset Valley to Franconia Notch or maybe over the highlands along the Ammonoosuc River to Fabyan's and the base of Mount Washington.

This brief introduction of the marvels of Mount Washington is intended to celebrate the early folklore and legends of the White Mountains; the first settlers and early passenger trains to invade the landscape of the North Country; and the first paths and roads to the summit of Mount Washington, including the Cog Railway and the Auto (Carriage) Road. Here we shall examine Sylvester Marsh's first proposal for a Cog Railway into the Granite State and the rail service to the summit of the mountain from 1869 to the present.

Finally, we will enjoy the natural splendor, the historic charm and the richness of the most beautiful scenery in the Northeast from the summit of Mount Washington. We will make a visit to a staffed observatory and the visitors' center, as well as the famous Tip-Top House. The top of the mountain will be memorable, for we shall experience the 360-degree views. We'll see hundreds of mountain peaks across three states and two countries and the possible shimmer of the faraway Atlantic Ocean.

A trip on the "Cog" up Mount Washington is more than an adventure; it is a virtual celebration of Nature's beauty.

LEGEND, FOLKLORE AND ORIGIN

OF MOUNT WASHINGTON

Early legends and myths of the White Mountains have been written by unnamed historians who have eloquently related them to us. Native Americans were natural storytellers. Seeing, as they did, an omen in every shifting shade of the clouds, a sign in the changing leaf, a token of beauty or ugliness in the different places of the wild and no rock or river, lake or mountain, valley or hillside that did not speak of some deed of valor or incident of love or hatred, these stories clung to their tongues and were told and retold to each succeeding generation. They were further kept alive by a name applied to a particular spot, which should always hint of the legend connected with it.

The Native Americans told their tales of bygone days with lowered voice and anxious mien, each myth fraught with the fantasy of nature's solitude and each legend bordered with a tinge of the silver foam of spirituality.

The following example of Native American myth and legacy of spirituality is related to us by an unknown historian:

> *In olden times, from far and near have come the brave and fair red children of the wilderness, to offer, in wild, shadowy glens, their sacrifices of vengeance and love, and where their songs rose, with the echoes of the thundering waterfalls, to mingle with the roaring wind of the tempest cloud, upon the snowy-crowned rocks, there they reverently believed the Great Spirit listening with satisfaction to their tribute of esteem. When the first white settlers came here to climb to the top of this bald mountain, an old Indian, with his tomahawk of stone, flint-pointed arrow, and tanned war dress, from the*

skins of moose and bear, standing proudly erect, shook his head, and said, "The Great Spirit dwells there; he covers steps above the green leaves with the darkness of the fire tempest. No footmarks are seen returning from his home in the clouds."

Not often did the Native Americans climb the mountains, but when they did, it was to save time and shorten distance. It was a difficult ascent for moccasined feet to climb over the stones and through the *hackmatacks*, as they called the dwarf firs and spruces, but on the bald mountain crest the way was easier.

William Little, in *The White Mountains*, continues our narrative:

When they reached the summit, the heaven, Kesuk, *was cloudless, and the view was unobstructed, it was a sight the like of which they had never seen before. Great mountains,* Wadchu, *were piled and scattered in its wildest state over the land, and silver lakes.* Sipes *were sparkling, bright rivers,* Sepoes *were gleaming from the dense forest below.*

As they sat upon the summit peak, the wind was still, and they could hear the moose bellowing in the gorges below; could hear the wolf, Muqoushim *howling; and now and then the Great War eagle of the mountains,* Keneu, *screamed and hurtled through the air. It was a feeling of revenge, which took possession of these Native Americans as they drank in the strange sights and wild primitive sounds, for they believed that the summit was the home of* Gitche Manitos, *their Great Spirit. The untutored Indian was filled with awe, as he stood in the dwelling-place of his God, afraid that the deity would be angry at the almost sacrilegious invasion.*

As the sun, Nepauz, *was going down in the western sky, a light mist collected around the eastern peaks, and above all the river valleys in the west, clouds assembled. First, no longer than a man's hand, but soon hanging over every valley was the assembly of showers—the heavens above them clear—the sun shining brightly upon the vapors. Quickly the winds freshened, and the great clouds, purple and gold and crimson above, were black as ink below, hurried from every quarter towards the summit of Mount Washington. Then thunder,* Pahtuquohan, *began to bellow, and the lightning,* Ukkutshaumon, *leaped from cloud to cloud, and* streas *of blinding rays shot down to the hills beneath, which the rain and hailstones, crashed upon the infinite thick woodland sent up a roar as a hundred mountain torrents. "It is* Gitche Manito *coming to his home angry,"* muttered [the Indian], *as with his companion*

Climbing the White Mountains of New Hampshire

he hurried down the mountain to the thick spruce for shelter for lasting protection of the Great Spirit.

Another Native American legend that has been passed down to us by Ernest E. Bisbee in his *White Mountain Scrapbook* presents stories and legends of the Crystal Hills of New Hampshire:

Once, during a dream of a famished Indian hunter the Great Spirit appeared to him, bestowing a flint-pointed spear and a dry coal by means of which he could secure food and fire. From the coal there came one night a flame, with blinding smoke and thunderous noise as a vast mountainous pile of broken rocks, which rose up at once, and from the flame a voice came saying, "Here the Great Spirit will dwell and watch over his favorite children." Thus arose the majestic Mt. Washington.

A third legend, known as the Deluge, said that many moons ago the entire world was destroyed—the White Mountains alone being excepted—by a great flood sent by the displeased Manitou. A great chieftain, who was considered a priest by his followers, and his wife fled to the mountains and by the aid of the Manitou were lifted to the summit of the cloud-piercing *Agiocochook*. They brought with them a hare, which after many nights was released and scampered down the mountainside, returning after a time with dry grass blades in its mouth. The chieftain and his wife descended the mountain and, finding the deluge over, built a tepee, where they lived for many years and raised many children, from whom came the Abenaki Indians.

A fourth legend tells of one of the great chieftains of the White Mountain region, Passaconaway, whose leadership probably antedated the landing of the first settlers in Plymouth, as he was seen by Captain Levett in 1623. In 1647, Passaconaway had a visit from the Reverend John Eliot and he and his sons were converted to Christianity. When and how he died is unknown, but tradition has it that he was drawn to the summit of Mount Washington in a sleigh by wolves, whence he ascended into heaven, Elijah-like, in a chariot of fire:

And once upon a car of flaming fire,
The dreadful Indian shook with fear to see
The king of Penacook, his chief, his sire,
Ride flaming up towards heaven, then
Any mountain higher.

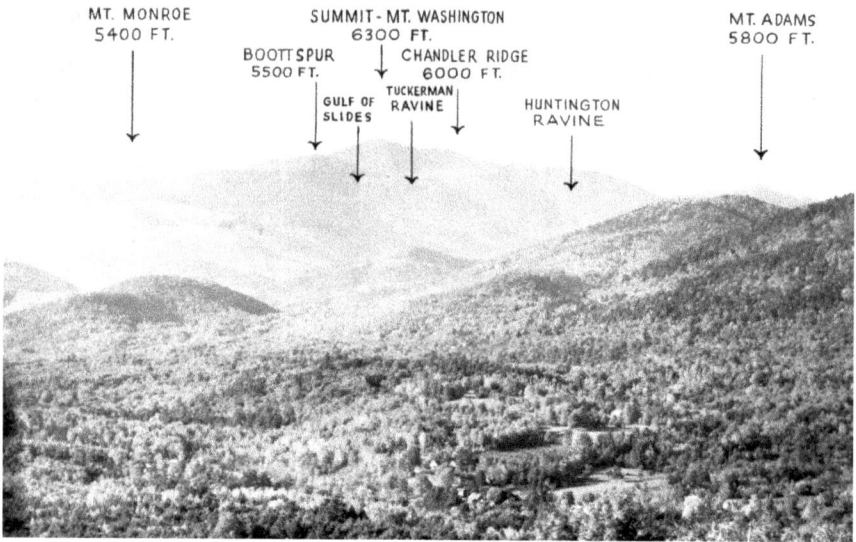

| MT. MONROE 5400 FT. | SUMMIT - MT. WASHINGTON 6300 FT. | | | MT. ADAMS 5800 FT. |

BOOTT SPUR 5500 FT.   CHANDLER RIDGE 6000 FT.

GULF OF SLIDES   TUCKERMAN RAVINE   HUNTINGTON RAVINE

The Presidential Range from Mount Cranmore in North Conway, New Hampshire, circa mid-1800s.

These traditions supported the fact that the Native Americans of these valleys were not mountain climbers and looked with reverence on the high peaks, considering them the home of superior spiritual beings. Consequently, ascending these peaks was considered extremely sacrilegious. The summit of Mount Washington was regarded with special veneration as the home of the Great Spirit.

NAMING THE MOUNTAIN

New England's highest peak has not always been known as Mount Washington. The aboriginal name was *Agiocochook*, or *Agiochook*, as it was sometimes spelled. This was, of course, a Native American name. Although applying to the entire range rather than to any particular summit, the name later referred to Mount Washington alone.

Another name was *Waumbekket-Menthna*. *Waumbekket* signifies "white" and *menthna*, "mountains." This, too, appeared in various contractions and spellings, and from it comes the name Waumbek.

The mountains were objects of respect, if not veneration, to those who settled under the shadow of their dominion. The White Mountains not only

14

Climbing the White Mountains of New Hampshire

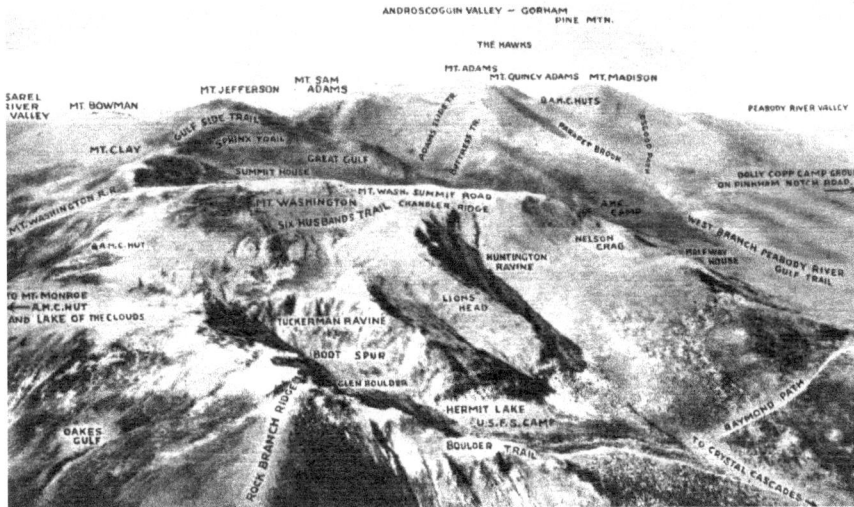

Mount Washington and the northern peaks of the Presidential Range in the White Mountains, including their names.

protect settlers from the biting blasts of the northlands, but they also unfold from their lofty summits the very scroll of nature's handiwork. The spirit of the mountain has always been the song of hope and freedom.

The Appalachian chain of highlands, following the Atlantic coast, finds its loftiest elevation and its strongest perfection in the White Mountains of New Hampshire. This series of mountains is about fifteen miles in length with Mount Washington as its central figure.

The majestic mountain summits were looked upon as hallowed retreats, where it was believed only the chosen of the Great Spirits could ascend. Their name for the highest was *Agiochook*, which meant "Home of the Great Spirit."

A popular name, not of Indian origin, was that of "Christall Hill," as found in a publication from 1628. This also appears in various forms and spellings, and from it came the term Crystal Hills.

A name that is not at all familiar but once ascribed to this grand summit is Trinity Height. Mention is made of this in the *Crawford History* pamphlet published in 1845 and occasionally elsewhere.

Now the nomenclature is gone, and with it fled the romance of the mountain and forest. More is the pity, until we can only say with Hiawatha:

Snow-capped Mount Washington in the White Mountains, as seen from Intervale. The most beautiful features of this landscape may be found in the rich verdure and charm of its surroundings, where the southern Presidential Range fills the horizon.

Lo! All things fade and perish!
From the memory of the old man
Fade away the great traditions,
The achievements of the warriors,
The adventures of the hunter.

In July 1784, the present name, Mount Washington, was probably given to this highest peak in the range in honor of the father of our country. Members of the first party to visit the mountain for scientific purposes were Reverend Dr. Jeremy Belknap, historian of New Hampshire, as the leading spirit, accompanied by Reverend Manasseh Cutler of Ipswich, Massachusetts; Reverend Daniel Little of Kennebunk, a physician; and three other men. Dr. Belknap, due to physical infirmity, was unable to climb the mountain, but he has left in his journal and in his *History of New Hampshire* a full record of the experiences of his companions. The party spent a night on the summit—doubtless the first mortals to do so—with no protection other than a fire during a night of rain. Dr. Cutler was probably the first visitor to write about the botany of Mount Washington. Cutler's River, which flows from Tuckerman's Ravine, was named for Dr. Cutler by his comrades on this mountain trip.

THE FIRST EXPLORER

Darby Field, of Exeter, New Hampshire, has been given the credit for being the first man to ascend and reach the summit of Mount Washington, a feat he accomplished twice in the year 1642. His first ascent was probably on June 4 of that year. The route was likely up over the Boott Spur Ridge along the southern side of Tuckerman's Ravine. Only two of his several Indian helpers could muster courage to master their superstitions and accompany him to the top.

Winthrop's account of the trip, in the quaint language of the day, was as follows:

> *They went with haste through the thick clouds for a good space, and within four miles of the top they had no clouds, but very cold. By the way, among the rocks, there were two ponds, one of blackish water and the other reddish. The top of all was a plain about sixty feet square. On the north side was a precipice, as they could scarcely discern to the bottom. They had neither cloud nor wind at the top, and moderate heat. All the country about him seemed a level, except here and there a hill rising above the rest, but far beneath them. He saw to the north, great water, which he judged to be 100 miles broad, but could see no land beyond it. The sea by Saco seemed as if it had been within twenty miles. He also saw a great sea to the eastward, which he judged to be the gulf of Canada. He saw great waters in parts to the westward, which he judged to be the great lakes, which Canada River comes out of. He found rare glass, they could dive out pieces forty feet long and seven or eight broad.*

It is now evident that Darby must have mistaken clouds or fog that he saw below him for large bodies of water, a natural mistake. After picking some "crystals" and shining stones, he and his companions descended the mountain and found the rest of the party drying their clothes beside a fire of pine knots, there having been a heavy thundershower in their absence. The Indians were very much astonished to see them come back safely, as they were sure the thunder and lightning had been sent by the Great Spirit to destroy Darby and his two companions for their audacity in trespassing on the sacred confines of *Agiochook*.

Josselyn's Account

The glowing reports that Darby Field spread about the riches to be found in the mountains spurred others to explore, and that same year Thomas, deputy governor of the colony, made the ascent. But as an early report had it, he found nothing worth his pain. John Josselyn, in 1672, gave an account of his exploration in his *New England Rarities Discovered*, from which the following is quoted:

> *From the rocky hill you may see the whole country round about; it is far above the lower cloud and from hence we beheld a mist drawn up by the sun beams out of a great lake, or pond into the air, where it was formed into a cloud. The country beyond these hills northward is daunted terrible, being full of rock hills, as thick as mole-hills in a meadow, and clothed with infinite thick woods.*

The First Path to the Summit

The first path to the summit was made in 1819 by Ethan Allen Crawford and assisted by his father, Abel Crawford. The ascent started from a point near where the Crawford House once stood by the railroad station, then went directly up Mount Clinton and along the range to the summit of Mountain Washington. In 1838–40, Ethan's brother, Thomas Crawford, improved the path and widened it into a road for horses to travel to the top of Mount Washington. Even though it is no longer traveled by horse, it is still known as the Crawford Bridle Path and is now maintained by the White Mountain National Forest.

In the summer of 1820, Thomas Crawford took a party of six gentlemen from Lancaster and Mr. Carrigain, an important state official, to the summit of Mount Washington to christen it. Leaving the Giant's Grave on horseback, they rode to the "Gate of the Notch" and then climbed up by foot about three miles, where they made camp. Ethan was "loaded like a pack horse," as he afterward related, with blankets, food and plenty of "Black Betts" or "O-be-joyful" to help in the christening. Continuing the next day, they stopped briefly at the Lake of the Clouds and then went on to the summit. It was a beautiful day, and as they named the several peaks, they drank toasts to the illustrious men for whom they were named.

Climbing the White Mountains of New Hampshire

The first path to the mountain by Ethan Allen Crawford would most likely have started at Crawford Notch. The deep pass through the notch is approximately three miles long and lies between Mount Willard on the west and Mounts Webster and Jackson on the east. It is commonly known as the "Gate to the Notch."

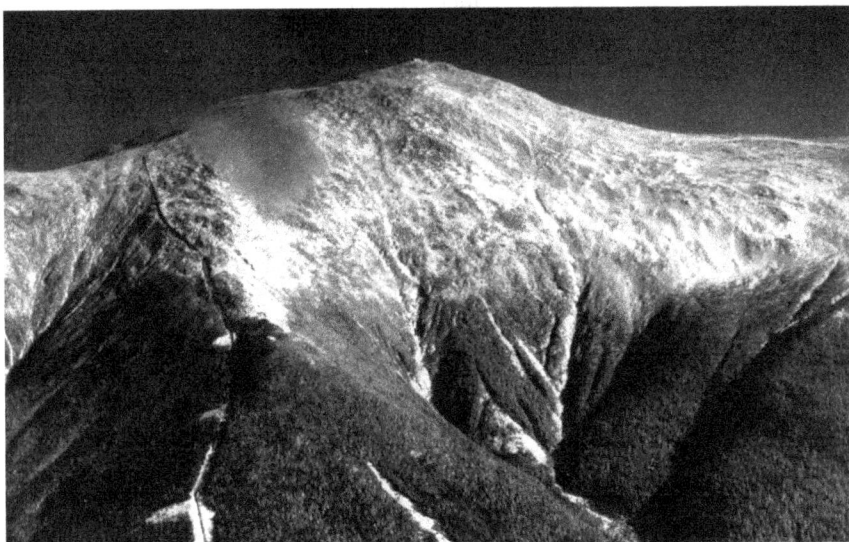

This is a striking aerial view of the Ammonoosuc Ravine and the Cog Railway on Mount Washington. On the far left is Burt Ravine.

The Davis Trail, reopened by the Appalachian Mountain Club, was first cut out about 1846 to accommodate travelers coming over the Tenth New Hampshire Turnpike, but owing to its excessive length and steep grade, it did not prove successful.

In a short time, the eastern route became much more popular, and the larger part of travelers found their way to Mount Washington by way of the town of Gorham. For many years before the advent of the Atlantic and Saint Lawrence Railroad, later known as the Grand Trunk, the Alpine House was known to travelers as the Gate of the White Mountain. When, about 1850, the railroad approached Gorham, mountain travel was increased, and in 1852, when the road was completed to that town, Gorham almost began to enjoy a monopoly of the mountain-climbing class of tourists.

At that time, the means of access to the summit from the Gorham side consisted of a path leading up through Tuckerman's Ravine. Over this path, and those from the Crawford side, so many made the ascent that the construction of a modest hotel on the summit was completed in 1851. Encouraged by the increased rush of travelers over the new railroad being developed through the White Mountains, the Glen House appeared in 1852, and soon afterward the proprietor of that hostelry cut out a bridle path to the summit over which he maintained a lucrative business with saddle horses for several years. Soon, the turnpike idea invaded the solitudes.

In December 1858, an early ascent of Mount Washington was made for business reasons, not for pleasure. Lucius Hartshorn, sheriff of Lancaster, was engaged by his father-in-law, one of the proprietors of the Tip-Top House, to attach some property at the summit, which was the subject of litigation. Hartshorn secured the services of B.F. Osgood of the Glen House, a very noted guide at the time, and together they went up the carriage road as far as the Halfway House. They went the rest of the way over the crusted snow. Finding themselves unable to force one of the doors off the building, they finally crawled through a window, on which the frost was a foot and a half thick. Inside, the walls and furniture had a covering of four inches of frost, and it was so dark that they had to light a lamp to see.

Upon leaving the hotel, they noted a frost cloud moving toward them with rapidity, and they just managed to reach the timberline and a little shelter before they were enveloped, which probably saved their lives. From here, they had no great difficulty in reaching the Glen House.

In the late fall of 1870, J.H. Huntington, of the State Geological Survey, who had successfully spent the preceding winter on Mount Moosilauke, made plans to stay on Mount Washington for the winter. He obtained

The Halfway House as seen during the early days of the Carriage (Auto) Road on the east side of Mount Washington.

permission from the Cog Railway to use its engine house at the summit and fitted out a special room to accommodate himself and several other observers. Mr. Huntington moved in on November 12, and the others came up at different times later in the season. The lowest temperature recorded that winter was fifty-nine degrees below zero, and the greatest wind velocity was estimated at 120 miles per hour. The provisions froze so hard that by February it was about as much of a job to saw off a chuck of salt pork as it would have been to cut a piece of marble. By keeping two fires going in their small apartment at red heat all night, they managed to exist but not keep warm. For most of the night, the noise of the wind outside prevented any of the party from sleeping.

The expedition excited great interest throughout the country, and the daily reports of the weather, sent over a newly laid telegraph line down the mountain, were watched with great interest.

2

THE FIRST ROAD TO THE SUMMIT

Today, the Carriage (Auto) Road is located on the east side of Mount Washington in Pinkham Notch. The first and only Carriage (Auto) Road leads up the mountain from the Glen House, a distance of eight miles, making an ascent of forty-six hundred feet, the usual grade being one foot in eight.

Building the road was an enormous task. The nearest source of supplies was eight miles away, and all transportation was by horse, oxen or on the backs of men.

On July 1, 1853, New Hampshire governor Noah Martin signed the bill of charter for the Mount Washington Road, an enterprise for which General David O. Macomber was initially responsible. To General Macomber belongs the credit for undertaking the building of the road, which was begun in 1855 and finished to the Halfway House. The next year, the company failed. Under a new company incorporated a few years later, work was resumed and was pushed with so much energy that within two years the road was completed for half its length. The financial difficulties stopped the work, and in 1858 the corporation was obliged to ask for an extension of its time. The New Hampshire legislature allowed the completion of the road to extend until August 1, 1861, but the difficulties into which the company had fallen were too great for that remedy. The Mount Washington Road Company gave up its existence.

In 1853, the Mount Washington Road Company was incorporated with turnpike privileges to build from the Peabody River Valley, over the top of Mount Washington, to a point between the Notch and Cherry Mountain.

The first road to the summit during the nineteenth century may have seen these summer tourists ascending the mountain on the Carriage Road via horse. This is an equestrian group on Mount Washington, July 1869, as conceived by illustrator Winslow Homer.

The corporation was organized in the same year at a meeting held in Gorham, and the route was surveyed in 1854.

In 1859, the Mount Washington Summit Road Company was created and was allowed a route the same as that of the earlier company. It took over the completed portion of the road and built the remaining road, giving access to the summit by carriage on August 8, 1861.

ASCENDING THE MOUNTAIN ON THE CARRIAGE (AUTO) ROAD

Under the franchise of 1859, the Carriage Road up Mount Washington is still in operation. For the first four miles, it winds through the ravine and over the eastern side of the mountain. The grade is easy and the roadbed excellent. Each turn discloses some new view—a wide valley faintly green, with a brook or a river flashing through it; a deep valley, with a swaying sea of foliage; an overhanging cliff that seems to render impossible any further ascent; or a wonderful array of peaks. Approaching the halfway point, the limit of vegetation is visible, and for half a mile or so the road appears to be the dividing line, the growth on the lower side being noticeably heavier. Emerging from the timber at the ledge near the Halfway House, the road continues in the same northerly direction for about half a mile, then widens and starts on its long climb up the crest of Chandler Ridge. As soon as the obstruction of the trees is removed, a succession of magnificent vistas are open to the eye: the northern peaks of the White Mountain Range, Jefferson, Adams and Madison, and of the Great Gulf, which lies between them and Mount Washington. Nearing the summit, the road skirts the edge of a sharp declivity, overlooking the Alpine Garden and Huntington Ravine, where the popular spring skiing presently takes place.

In its length of eight miles, the Auto Road makes the ascent from an elevation of 1,543 feet above sea level to an altitude of 6,288 feet, the highest point in New England. The average grade is seen to be 594 feet to the mile, while the maximum grade is said to be at the rate of 880 feet.

The memory of John P. Rich, one of the unlucky contractors under the first company and superintendent of construction for the second, is perpetuated by a memorial tablet set by the road near the base of the mountain. Others to whom credit for this bold enterprise and achievement is due include David O. Macomber of Middletown, Connecticut, the projector of the scheme and first president of the corporation, and C.H.V. Davis, to whose engineering skills are due the practical grades by which the summit is reached.

On account of the deep cliffs almost under the passenger's elbow, and the possibility of a frightful accident, great care has always been exercised by the management in the selection of its drivers, and only extra strong and steady horses with specially built vehicles were used. Consequently, one accident in which a passenger was killed lies to the charge of the company. In the summer of 1880, a wagon carrying nine people down the mountain upset at a sharp turn in the road about a mile below the Halfway House, throwing the passengers onto the rocks, killing one and injuring all the others.

On August 8, 1861, the day of the opening of the carriage road, the first passenger vehicle ever to ascend Mount Washington was an old-fashioned Concord state coach, drawn by eight horses and driven by George W. Lane. Never again was one of these cumbrous vehicles driven to the summit, save in 1899, and then simply as a movie stunt planned by B.F. Keith. Ever since this road became suitable for the automobile, the Carriage Road has become the predominant means of travel for over 150,00 people a year to ascend the mountain.

Climbing the White Mountains of New Hampshire

This is an excellent view of the northern peaks of the Presidential Range as seen from the Carriage Road. From left to right are Mounts Jefferson, Adams and Madison.

The summit of Mount Washington as imagined by the projectors of the Carriage Road.

A group of tourists in their four-horse stage are preparing for the ascent up the Carriage Road to the summit of Mount Washington. The carriage driver was often also innkeeper of the local house, such as Landlord Thompson of the Glen House.

Until the railway came, the Carriage Road was the principal route to the summit, and it has never ceased to be a popular road. For many years, a fleet of mountain wagons, carrying either nine or twelve persons and drawn by four or six horses, often brought up fifty and sometimes one hundred passengers in a day. Many of the landlords from local hotels and inns of that time were expert drivers, and the ride with them to the summit was one of the events of every season in which their guests took the keenest pleasure.

EVENTS

The first auto to ever take the climb was a Stanley Steamer, driven by F.O. Stanley, who made the ascent on August 31, 1899, accompanied by his wife, in two hours and ten minutes. The first officially timed auto ascent was made on August 25, 1903, the time being one hour and forty-six minutes. A year later, on July 11–12, 1904, was held the first contest known as the Climb to the Clouds, which was won by a Mercedes car driven by Harry Harkness of New York, in twenty-four minutes, thirty-seven and three-fifths seconds. In the second contest, held on July 17–18, 1905, all previous records were broken by W.M. Hilliard in a Napler car, in twenty minutes,

Climbing the White Mountains of New Hampshire

After an eight-hour climb on April 3, 1932, with a team of five Eskimo sled dogs, Mrs. Florence Clark's third attempt to reach the top of Mount Washington was successful.

fifty-eight and two-fifths seconds. In 1923, Ralph Mulford, driving a touring car, established a new record of seventeen minutes flat. This was not broken until September 21, 1928, when Cannon Ball Baker, in a Franklin Special, successfully rounded the more than eighty curves on this eight-mile stone and gravel choppy road, with its 4,673 feet of rise at grades from 12 to 26 percent, in fourteen minutes, forty-nine and three-fifths seconds.

Every year in June, the mountain road is host to the Mount Washington Road Race, which attracts hundreds of runners. In July, the mountain road hosts Newton's Revenge and in August, the Mount Washington Auto Road Bicycle Hill Climb, both of which are bicycle races that run the same route as the road race.

After eight hours of climbing Mount Washington, Florence Clark's third, and successful, attempt to drive a team of five Eskimo sled dogs to the top of the mountain was achieved. The day was April 3, 1932. She was the first woman to drive a sled dog team to the summit of Mount Washington and back. She is pictured with her team and Clackso, her female lead dog, which led the team of five dogs during the climb to the summit.

Celebrating 150 years in 2011, the Mount Washington Auto Road is indeed an American icon.

3

Railroads to the Granite State

B y 1835, the stagecoach system and the river boating companies were well established, and New Hampshire folks were well off as far as transportation was concerned. They paid little attention to any rumors about steam railroads, which were being built in southern New England. Then, in a few years, there was talk of running a railroad into New Hampshire. People everywhere fought the idea. They said these funny little engines and their trains with little cars would scare the cows, stop the hens from laying and set fire to the fields and forest. But the railroad came just the same.

Just as the changeover was taking place, numerous aspersions were naturally cast on the railroads of New England, primarily for doing away with the stage companies, the local taverns, the large stables and their occupants, blacksmith shops, etc. This change came more quickly than the switch from the sailing ship to steamship. It was claimed that most of the horses would have to be killed, as they were no longer useful for travel.

Alice Morse Earle wrote in *Stage Coach and Tavern Days* that someone declared:

> *There would therefore by no market for oats or hay. Hens would not lay eggs on account of the noise. It would cause insanity. There would be constant fires from the sparks from the engines. It was declared that no car could ever advance against the wind.*

The first train ever seen in New Hampshire chugged into Nashua from Lowell one day in 1838, and a new era had begun. It is interesting to note that this first railroad ran right along the Merrimack River, where the river freight boats had been operating for nearly thirty years. The boat people might have wondered if this new plaything would eventually compete with them, but no one thought so in 1838. Four years later, the railroad had been extended to Concord, and the little trains were proving that they could haul more freight faster and cheaper than riverboats, wagons and oxcarts. It was because most of New Hampshire's growing factories were located in the Merrimack Valley that the first railroad was built in that valley. The railroads, in turn, helped the factories grow at a faster rate.

The railroads were built very quickly in our state. In 1841, a line from Boston into Maine was completed, running through Portsmouth. The Northern Railroad Company built a line in 1846 from Concord to Franklin, and two years later a line had been extended to reach Lebanon and the Connecticut River. Keene had a railroad come in from the south in 1849, and Exeter was linked to Haverhill, Massachusetts, by rail that same year. A year later, the Exeter line had been pushed north to Dover. Meanwhile, the Boston, Concord & Montreal Railroad was moving north, reaching Tilton in 1848, Meredith in 1849, Plymouth by the next year, Warren in 1851 and Woodstock by 1853.

The railroads killed the picturesque river traffic almost immediately, as well as some of the stage routes. However, the railroads were built only through the larger towns and cities, leaving many acres of the state just as they were, with only wagons and coaches for transportation. The stagecoaches continued to be used for many years in the state, although in reduced numbers. In fact, the last stages didn't disappear until they were replaced by automobiles and buses in the twentieth century.

The new railroads not only carried freight, but they also carried passengers and soon took over the job of carrying mail and express. With an improved mail service, the publication of newspapers and magazines began to spread. By the middle of the nineteenth century, a few years before the Civil War, most of the larger cities in New Hampshire had their own newspapers, and several national magazines had been established, and copies were found in New Hampshire homes. People no longer felt cut off from the next town and the rest of the world. Then, in 1844, Morse invented the telegraph. Like the railroads, this was considered a toy at first, but soon wires began to appear along the railroad tracks. People in Concord could know what was happening in New York five minutes after it happened.

The White Mountain Railroad was chartered on December 24, 1848, and opened to Littleton in 1853. In 1858, by authority of an act of the New

The Fabyan House, near the base of Mount Washington, was the beginning route from the Mount Washington Turnpike Company to the foot of the mountain. This station was the most important point in the mountain district for all the Boston and New York express trains.

Hampshire legislature, the White Mountain Railroad was sold at auction for $24,000 and debts. It was auctioned off by mortgage holders, who organized a new company under the name White Mountain New Hampshire Railroad. The road was at once leased to the Boston, Concord & Montreal Railroad for $12,000 in 1864, and the lease extended twenty years. This rental was about sufficient to pay the interest on the debt.

In 1869, the construction of an extension of the White Mountain Railroad beyond Littleton was undertaken, and in 1872 the track from Wing Road toward the base of Mount Washington was begun. However, in 1883 the construction account of the line from Wing Road to the base of Mount Washington was closed. In June 1, 1883, this road was leased to the Boston & Lowell Railroad.

On May 1, 1889, the lease to the Boston & Lowell was declared void, and the road was at once consolidated with the Concord Railroad under the name of the Concord & Montreal Railroad. In 1895, the Concord & Montreal system was leased by the Boston & Maine Railroad system, thus gaining control of the spur, which connected directly from the Fabyan House to the base of Mount Washington.

At the beginning of the twentieth century, the Boston & Maine operated on 2,324 miles of track—a product of consolidating forty-seven major and minor independent lines in central and northern New England.

Climbing the White Mountains of New Hampshire

In 1893, A. Alexander McLeod assumed the presidency of the Boston & Maine and quickly managed to lease the Connecticut River Railroad, a line that was coveted by the New York, New Haven & Hartford Railroad and J.P. Morgan. Mr. Morgan stabilized the situation by imposing a settlement between the Boston & Maine and the New York, New Haven & Hartford lines. The settlement removed McLeod from his presidency, and Lusius Tuttle (formally of the New York, New Haven & Hartford Railroad) became the new president. Before the end of the nineteenth century, Tuttle was able, in 1895, to lease the 424 miles of the Concord & Montreal Railroad.

During the process of consolidation, virtually all New Hampshire's railroad corporations disappeared or ceased operating independently. By 1905, there were fourteen miles of railroad to each one hundred square miles of territory and a mile of railroad to every 350 inhabitants. As a result of further consolidation and litigation, the Mount Washington Railway came under the control of the Boston & Maine Railroad system.

Due to a major fire at the base in 1895, which destroyed all the building and facilities except the Marshfield House, the Boston & Maine decided to rebuild the facilities. In 1897, a new engine house, a car shed, a transform platform, a fuel shed and a boardinghouse for railway employees were built. Two locomotives, the Eagle and the Cloud, were damaged in the fire. They were scrapped. Two others, the Atlas and the Tip-Top, were rebuilt.

Boston & Maine Locomotive No. 50 (4-4-0) at the base of Mount Washington, second transfer station, circa 1900. The Boston & Maine Railroad leased this line connecting the Cog Railway base station with Fabyan's station.

THE MOUNT WASHINGTON COG RAILWAY

The decline of branch line railroads between 1915 and 1926 was due primarily to competition of motor vehicles and increasing price of labor and fuel. From this point on, the Boston & Maine began to lose its grip on its own railroad. Early in the twentieth century, the Boston & Maine was temporarily absorbed by the New York, New Haven & Hartford Railroad, which was under the control of J.P. Morgan. During the Great Depression, and in the years following, the Boston & Maine had difficulties supporting its passenger service, primarily tourists to the White Mountains. The railroads were forced to discontinue service. In 1969, the Boston & Maine declared bankruptcy. The golden era of the railroad had ended, but their legacy lives on today.

THE MOUNT WASHINGTON TURNPIKE

A successful venture was that of the Mount Washington Turnpike Company, which was chartered in 1867 and was allowed a route extending from the Fabyan House to the foot of Mount Washington. That was several miles from the nearest road, the Tenth New Hampshire Turnpike, while the nearest railroad station was at Littleton, twenty-five miles away. So the turnpike was conceived as a means of transporting to the site of the new railroad the various supplies necessary for its construction and equipment and later to derive a profit from the tolls collected from tourists on their way to the mountain.

The profitable life of this turnpike was destined to be short, for summer travel to the White Mountains was growing very popular, and it was unlikely that the railroads would long leave such a lucrative field unoccupied. The Boston, Concord & Montreal Railroad was completed as far as Littleton when the turnpike was projected, and it lost no time in pushing nearer. But times were hard, and the construction proceeded by piecemeal. Between 1873 and 1876, the rails crept ahead a little at a time, until the Fabyan House was reached, after which the remaining five miles to the base were reached, and the whole length was opened for passengers on July 6, 1876.

But the turnpike still held on, and its rate-of-toll sign at Fabyan's was long a familiar object to tourists with its unique spacing. Many will recall the heading: "Rates of Toll on the Mt. Washington Turnpike."

The railroad must have felt the competition of the old-fashioned competitor, for early in 1882, a small block, three-eighths of the total of the capital stock, was bought by the directors of the Boston, Concord & Montreal Railroad, and later purchases resulted in the acquisition of it all.

In 1885, authority was secured from the legislature to extend the Mount Washington Turnpike, called in the act the White Mountain Turnpike, to a junction with the Mount Washington Summit Road, but the plan was never carried out.

Even the railroad managers could not make the turnpike a success, and they were glad to get rid of the road. On May 13, 1903, the turnpike was deeded to the State of New Hampshire.

4

Sylvester Marsh's Railway

The First Railway to the Summit

The story of Sylvester Marsh has been told many times, but there is an elaboration on him and his rail system. Marsh was born in Campton, New Hampshire, and did not see a wheeled vehicle in that community until the age of nine. He made his fortune in the Midwest. He returned to his native state in 1852 and made an ascent of Mount Washington. He set about to invent a railroad apparatus that would ascend the majestic summit of Mount Washington. In 1858, he obtained a charter for such an undertaking from the New Hampshire legislature.

After many years of persistent effort, in spite of ridicule and discouragement, Sylvester Marsh at last succeeded in raising capital for his plan to build a railroad up Mount Washington. The form of cars and locomotive to be used on the new road, being adapted to the steep grades, naturally was not suitable for operation on level ground, and the mountain-climbing railroad necessarily made its terminus at the foot of the mountain.

No doubt, the idea of a cog railroad to the summit of Mount Washington was something that appealed to a mechanical genius like Sylvester Marsh in its own right, but the reason, which he gave years later, was even more personal, as he testified before a Senate committee:

> *I built it for a pastime, and to cure the dyspepsia, more than anything else. I retired from business in 1855, and after living for a few years doing nothing I had dyspepsia very badly, and was compelled to do something to save my health. I got this idea into my head and worked upon it, and built different*

models of it until I worked it out. It was ridiculed a great deal and laughed at, but it cured my dyspepsia.

As one of the steps in the process of forwarding his railroad scheme, Sylvester Marsh applied for a patent. He was no stranger to the Patent Office, having invented devices for the mechanical handling of grain and grain dryers. Mr. Marsh, then living in West Roxbury, Massachusetts, made application on August 24, 1858, for improvements in locomotives for ascending planes. He appointed Ezra Lincoln as his agent. The application consisted of four legal-sized pages of description signed by Marsh and two witnesses.

On September 6, the Patent Office rejected his application, calling attention to similar patents of five persons ranging from 1836 to 1849. No doubt, this illustrates the truism that no invention is completely independent. The matter rested with the Patent Office until March. Through his attorney, Mr. A. Pollack, Marsh submitted an amendment on August 3, 1861, to the original 1858 specification. This amendment was substituted in the last paragraph. On this basis, the patent was issued on September 10, 1861, number 33255.

In 1866, Marsh took out another patent on the basic central rail. During the same year, a company was formed and construction began.

Sylvester Marsh accompanied his specification with diagrams on his invention, as well the manuscript version, which refers to this plate of diagrams. Mr. Marsh described his invention as follows:

The present invention related to that class of locomotives, which are used for ascending very steep grades, and has for its object, first, obtaining sufficient power to ascent a steep inclination with a light locomotive instead of a heavy and cumbersome one, such as have heretofore been necessarily used; second, preventing the possibility of the engine being thrown off or lifted and un-geared from the track by the interposition of any obstruction thereon, and the means employed for checking and stopping the progress of the train.

I will now proceed to describe in detail the construction of my improved locomotive:
a. in the drawings represent the outer rails of a railroad track on a steep grade.
b. is a central rail constructed with a gear-rack
c. and projecting flangs
e. represents the body of the locomotive

f. is the smoke-pipe

g. the steam-cylinder

h. an eccentric worked by the connecting-rod

i. running-wheels that support the locomotive upon the outer rails.

j.

k. is the driving shaft, driven by the connecting-rod.

l. attached to the eccentric

h. on the driving-shaft

k. is a pinion

m. that engages with a large gear-wheel

n. attached to the axle of the rear running-wheels

i. a gear n' on the same axle o works into the geared rack

c. on the central rail

b. and thus by a motion received from the pinion m drives the locomotive.

It had been customary in the construction of locomotives for ascending inclined planes to attach the connecting rod directly to the driving wheel of the locomotive, which of course necessitated the use of a large engine of great power, whereas by the arrangement above described, a light locomotive of small power could be successfully used. Sylvester Marsh provided the following data:

P is a lever-pawl, which is enraged with or disengaged from the gear n by means of a cam q, and serves to prevent the engine from running backward when engaged with the gear n and is disengaged with the gear n and is disengaged when the train is descending.

The rear n' is prevented from being lifted out of the geared rack cc of the central rail in case of any obstruction on the track by means of the small friction-wheel rr, attached to two spring-plates ss, which are made to bind upon and clasp the sides of the central rail at pleasure by means of an eccentric t (worked by a brake-rod u) which moves two short levers v (connected by a rod w) the ends of which abut against one of the spring-plates s, and are attached to the bars xx, which play through the spring-plate and draw them together when the brake-rod u is turned in the proper direction, as will readily be understood by inspection of Figs, 3, 4, and 5. The importance of this arrangement of holding the engine upon the track by the spring-plates and friction-rollers will be manifest, as the disengagement of the gear n' from the central rail would be attended with serious consequences. The progress of the train can also be checked or

UNITED STATES PATENT OFFICE.

SYLVESTER MARSH, OF WEST ROXBURY, MASSACHUSETTS.

IMPROVEMENT IN LOCOMOTIVE-ENGINES FOR ASCENDING INCLINED PLANES.

Specification forming part of Letters Patent No. **33,255**, dated September 10, 1861.

To all whom it may concern:

Be it known that I, SYLVESTER MARSH, of West Roxbury, in the county of Norfolk and State of Massachusetts, have invented certain new and useful Improvements in Locomotive-Engines for Ascending Inclined Planes; and I do hereby declare that the following description, taken in connection with the accompanying drawings, hereinafter referred to, forms a full and exact specification of the same, wherein I have set forth the nature and principles of my said improvements, by which my invention may be distinguished from all others of a similar class, together with such parts as I claim and desire to have secured to me by Letters Patent.

The figures of the accompanying plate of drawings represent my improvements.

Figure 1 is a side elevation of my improved locomotive-engine. Fig. 2 is a central longitudinal vertical section of the same. Fig. 3 is a section taken in the plane of the line A B, Fig. 1. Figs. 4, 5, and 6 are views in details to be hereinafter referred to.

The present invention relates to that class of locomotives which are used for ascending very steep grades, and has for its objects, first, obtaining sufficient power to ascend a steep inclination with a light locomotive instead of a heavy and cumbersome one, such as have heretofore been necessarily used; second, preventing the possibility of the engine being thrown off or lifted and ungeared from the track by the interposition of any obstruction thereon, and the means employed for checking and stopping the progress of the train.

I will now proceed to describe in detail the construction of my improved locomotive.

a a is the drawings represent the outer rails of a railroad-track on a steep grade.

b b is a central rail constructed with a gear-rack *c c* and projecting flanges *d d*.

f is the smoke-pipe; *g*, the steam-cylinder; *h*, an eccentric worked by the connecting-rod *l*; and *i i i i*, running-wheels that support the locomotive upon the outer rails *a a*.

k is the driving-shaft, driven by the connecting-rod *l*, attached to the eccentric *h*. On the driving-shaft *k* is a pinion *m*, that engages with a large gear-wheel *n*, attached to the

axle *g* of the rear running-wheels *i i*. A gear *n'* on the same axle *n* works into the geared rack *c c* on the central rail *b b*, and thus by the motion received from the pinion *m* drives the locomotive.

It has heretofore been customary in the construction of locomotives for ascending inclined planes to attach the connecting-rod directly to the driving-wheel of the locomotive, which of course necessitated the use of a large engine of great power, whereas by the arrangement above described a light locomotive of small power can be successfully used.

p is a lever-pawl, which is engaged with or disengaged from the gear *n* by means of a cam *q*, and serves to prevent the engine from running backward when engaged with the gear *n* and is disengaged when the train is descending.

The gear *n'* is prevented from being lifted out of the geared rack *c c* of the central rail in case of any obstruction on the track by means of the small friction-wheels *r r*, attached to two spring-plates *s s*, which are made to bind upon and clasp the sides of the central rail at pleasure by means of an eccentric *t*, (worked by a brake-rod *u*,) which moves two short levers *v*, (connected by a rod *w*,) the ends of which abut against one of the spring-plates *s*, and are attached to the bars *x x*, which play through the spring-plates and draw them together when the brake-rod *u* is turned in the proper direction, as will readily be understood by inspection of Figs. 3, 4, and 5. The importance of this arrangement of the spring-plates and friction-rollers will be manifest, as the disengagement of the gear *n'* from the central rail would be attended with serious consequences. The progress of the train can also be checked or stopped altogether by means of two levers *y y*, the ends of which are made to embrace both faces of the gear *n*, before referred to, by the turning of a cam *z*, actuated by a brake-rod *u'*, as will be readily understood by inspection of Fig. 6.

Having thus described my improvements, what I claim as new, and desire to secure by Letters Patent, is—

1. The general **1** herein described for inclined planes

consisting of the eccentric *h*, attached to the connecting-rod of the engine, the pinion *m*, and gears *n* and *n'*, in combination with a toothed central rail, as set forth.

2. In combination, with the central rail constructed with flanges, as described, the traveling friction-rollers and the spring-plates

arranged in relation to the devices operating them, in the manner and for the purposes set forth.

SYLVESTER MARSH.

Witnesses:
JOSEPH GAVETT,
ALBERT W. BROWN.

SYLVESTER MARSH'S RAILROAD

Page one of the document from the United States Patent Office issued to Sylvester Marsh of West Roxbury, Massachusetts, titled: "Improvement in Locomotive-Engines for Ascending Inclined Planes."

October 20, pointing out the patent of one Smith Cram for a cog rail as early as June 11, 1896. Again Marsh amended his description to cover this situation and the objection was withdrawn. The Patent Office[a] issued the letters patent on January 15, 1867.

One wonders how often the Patent Office has had an opportunity to share in a dyspepsia cure!

[a] Records of the Patent Office, National Archives, Patent No. 61221.

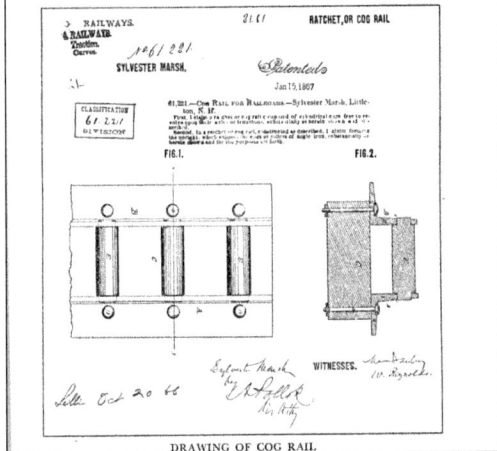

DRAWING OF COG RAIL

Page two of Sylvester Marsh's patent. *Railroad Records of the Patent Office, National Archives, Patent No. 61221.*

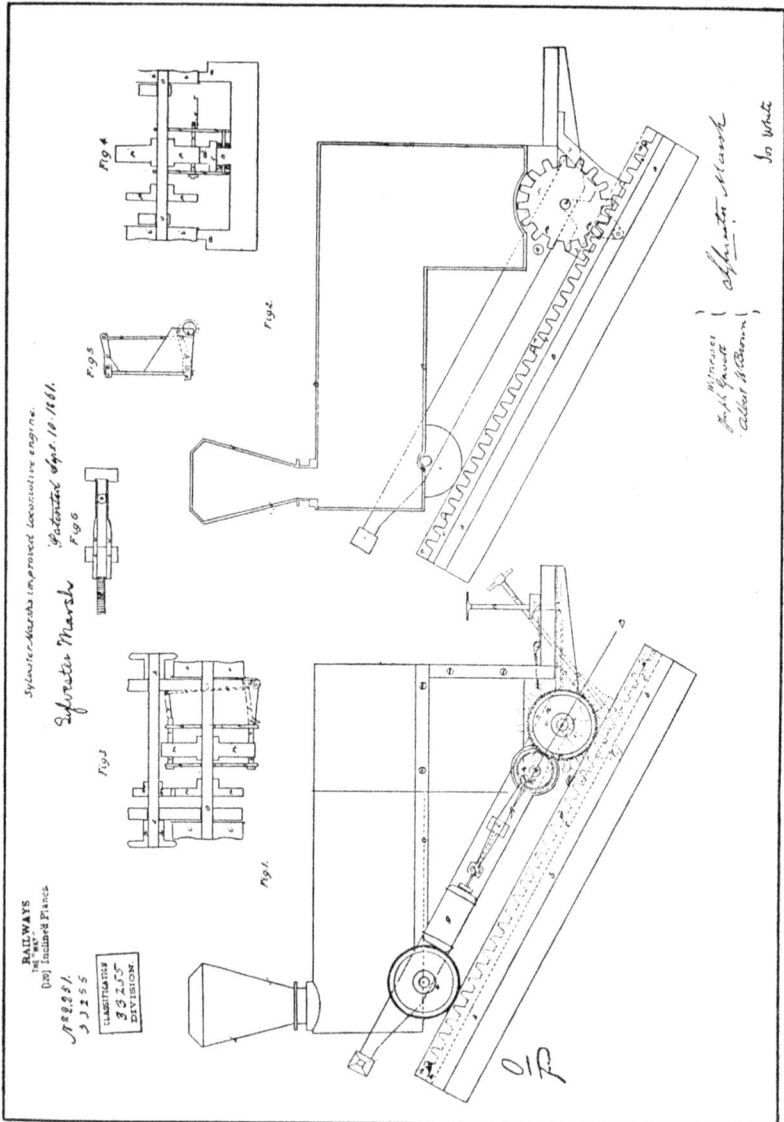

DRAWING OF COG-WHEEL LOCOMOTIVE

A drawing of the cogwheel locomotive, September 10, 1861.

stopped altogether by means of two levers yy, the ends of which are made to embrace both faces of the gear n, before referred to, by the turning of the cam z, actuated by the break-rod a', as will be readily understood by inspection of Fig. 6.

Climbing the White Mountains of New Hampshire

The original cog-road engine Old Peppersass, 1866. The original locomotive was christened the Hero. However, one old-timer thought it looked like a bottle of peppersass (pepper sauce), and thus the name Old Peppersass was born.

Having described my improvements, what I claim as my invention, and desire to have secured to me by letter, Patent, is:

1. The general arrangement of devices herein described from driving the locomotives on inclined planes of a steep grade, the same consisting of the eccentric h, attached to the connecting-rod of the engine, the pinion m, and gears n and n', in combination with the toothed central rail, as set forth.

2. In combination, with the central rail constructed with flanges, as described, the traveling friction-roller and the spring-plate arranged in relation to the devices operating them, in the manner and for the purposes set forth.

In 1858, Sylvester Marsh exhibited a model of his engine and cog railway to the New Hampshire state legislature. He was granted a charter to build a steam railway up Mount Washington and Mount Lafayette.

It is interesting to note that the vertical type of locomotive known as the Peppersauce (Old Peppersass) had some resemblance to the long-necked pepper sauce bottle. This was not contemplated in the drawing submitted by Mr. Marsh to the Patent Office but rather is the type of boiler now in use on the steam engine.

According to Guy Roberts and Frank H. Burt in their research on Sylvester Marsh, the following is recorded in their *Old Peppersass*:

> *The Mount Washington Steam Railway Company was finally organized by Sylvester Marsh, as President and Construction agent, and in 1866 it was completed as an organization with work commencing on the railway the following May. The directors were: Messrs. Marsh, Lyon, White, Keyes, and Upham. The stock for the company, being owned by the Boston and Maine Railroad, and the property, was operated separately. The entire construction was accomplished by July 1869.*

The company was financed to the extent of $20,000 as follows:

Sylvester Marsh	*$5,000*
John E. Lyon	*5,000*
Cheeney and Company	*2,500*
Rivers, or Passumpsic Rail Road, or Henry Keyes	*2,500*
Concord Railroad, by N.G. Upham	*2,500*
Northern Railroad, by Onslow Stearns	*1,000*
J.F. Marsh	*500*
	500
Pitman and Dodge of the B.C. and M. RR	*500*
Total	*20,000*

THE FIRST RAILWAY TO THE SUMMIT

Mr. Marsh's description of the actual building of the first part of the railroad on the mountain was quite interesting:

> *I had been over the mountain with my son, Frank, who is a civil engineer, and we surveyed the steepest part to ascertain its grade. Afterwards with the assistance of "Cal" Freeman of Lancaster, son-in-law of Ethan Allen Crawford, we surveyed different routes up the mountain and decided to start where the Marshfield Station Depot is located at the base of the mountain, near the Ammonoosuc River. At this time it was a dense forest with no track or road leading to it, except an old logging road from Fabyan's to within one-half mile of the place from which we were to start. From the end of the logging road, we blazed a trail and put up a log cabin, in the meantime*

Climbing the White Mountains of New Hampshire

The Cog Railway tracks are seen crossing the Ammonoosuc River near the base station of Mount Washington.

the men camped out. I drove oxen in, in single file and the men carried in the yoke, and we used the oxen to dray logs for the cabin. As soon as we had a place where men could stay, I had them stark hewing timber to begin the construction of the railroad. I next set the men to repair and widening the old logging road so that we could get in supplies and materials to the cabin with ox teams. I constructed a short piece of the railroad, about 40 rods, known as the "first test track" and then hauled in the engine, piece-meal. We then put up a temporary blacksmith shop, framed the engine and put it on the track. My next move was to build a platform car.

Work on the railway began in May 1866. Sylvester Marsh had already made contact with Campbell, Whittier and Company in Roxbury, Massachusetts, to build a geared steam locomotive. His son John, who worked with this company, supervised its construction.

The first locomotive, as devised by Mr. Marsh, resembled a hoisting engine, the boiler being upright instead of horizontal, and was without a cab. It also had one pair of cylinders and drive wheels instead of two pairs as engines now have. The locomotive and track were built on the "rack and pinion" principle. The rack was the middle, or "cog-rail," which consisted of two continuous-angle irons connected by heavy cross pins four inches

41

long and two and a half inches apart. This cog rail was securely bolted to the wooden framework of the roadbed and into it played, with perfect security, the heavy-toothed wheels under the engine, which was equipped with two pairs of cylinders. It was, in fact, a double engine, each pair operating independently of the other. On the cars, there were cogwheels and large friction brake wheels, which provide brakes of considerable power. The engines had a toothed ratchet wheel, and it was the clatter of this ratchet that could be heard constantly while ascending the mountain. While this may have become a bit monotonous, one could have felt perfectly safe so long as it clattered. In descending the mountain, powerful friction brakes operated by the brakeman help retard the car, and these in conjunction with still other brakes and safety appliances made the descent fully as safe as the ascent.

Some of these locomotives, as well as the earlier ones, built by the shops of Walter Aiken of Franklin, New Hampshire, had but one pair of cylinders, which, according to Glen M. Kidder, author of *Railway to the Moon,*

by gears powered one axle only—the front one in the case of locomotive No. 1, The "Hero." The locomotives constructed subsequently were more powerful as they were built with two pairs of cylinders, which doubled the amount of force propelling the locomotive and also increased the safety factor. In the Aiken-built locomotive, the power to the axle was based on a 4 to 1 ratio, that is, for each turn of the small driving gear, the gear meshing

The cog locomotive Waumbek in all its glory ascending the mountain at the skyline, July 1950.

with the cog rail turned one quarter of a revolution, thus producing a great amount of force (rate at 50 horsepower in the case of locomotive No. 2 "Geo. Stephenson" and the other Aiken-built locomotives) at the sacrifice of speed. As a result, their speed normally was limited to not more than 3 miles per hour.

Recent improvements in design have replaced the ratchet (gear and pawl mechanism) with Sprague clutches and disc brake assemblies. Many locomotives for the Mount Washington Railroad Company were made by the Manchester Locomotive Works in Manchester, New Hampshire, as well their own Mt. Washington Cog Railway Shop.

The present type of locomotive, with its horizontal boiler, lower in front, thus being nearly level when on the mountain, was a later development of Marsh and Aiken's, and two of these were built by Walter Aiken, of Franklin, New Hampshire, who worked out the practical details of Mr. Marsh's idea and supervised the construction of the road. In use, the car—one to an engine, with tilted seats for about forty passengers—is pushed up the mountain. In descending, the engine precedes the car, or backs down in front of it, thus ensuring greater safety.

BUILDING THE COG ROAD

The public in general refused to take Mr. Marsh's invention seriously, and funds for building the road were slow in arriving.

The first demonstration trip on the railway happened on August 29, 1866. It was then that the locomotive Hero, later known as Old Peppersass, pushed a flatcar up and down this new experimental track, which took better than two hours.

According to Glen M. Kidder in his *Railway to the Moon*:

The demonstration run was quite successful and it convinced those present that the idea was entirely feasible—that the locomotive not only could push a car loaded with passengers up a steep incline, but could stop almost instantaneously on a steep incline and be securely held there. It was also demonstrated that the loaded car could be lowered by gravity, entirely independent, as well as those built later, and stopped at will by hand braking.

Following the successful demonstration, there was afterward very little difficulty in securing further funds from the various interested railroads, and "Crazy Marsh's" idea was completed to Jacob's Ladder and formally opened on August 14, 1868.

Needless to say, the guests were so pleased with the demonstration that they passed resolutions, as published in Mount Washington in the winter of 1870–71, as follows:

> *Resolved: That we have witnessed with deep interest that trial run made this day on the railroad now being constructed to the summit of Mt. Washington, and would express our full confidence in the scientific principles of its construction and its practical and safe mode of operation.*
>
> *Resolved: The we regard the construction of this road as a new era in the application of steam power in overcoming grades over high summits and mountain ascents, so as to open new means of business enterprise and greatly enlarge the facilities of enjoyment of the best and noblest scenery of the country.*
>
> *Resolved: That Sylvester Marsh, by his great skill and ingenuity in the invention of his newly constructed mode of railway for ascending high grades, and his energy and efficiency in its practical application is entitled to the high appreciation and regard of his fellow citizens and is richly deserving our tribute to him as a public benefactor.*

Up until then, Sylvester Marsh had used his own money for the financing of the railway, but now, support for his endeavor was paying off.

The company was finally furnished, via the various interested railroads, with necessary funding and supplies. Thus, work began in 1866 and was completed in July 1869 at a cost of $139,500. The invention and building of this remarkable railroad is all the more remarkable when we realize that nearly all the material, and cars, had to be hauled by teams from Littleton, New Hampshire, the nearest railroad point, twenty-five miles away.

It may truly be stated that the cog road of the Mount Washington Cog Railway was the first mountain-climbing cog railway (rack-and-pinion railway) in the world. It is also the second steepest cog road in the world, as well as the oldest.

Historically, the railway was located in the Thompson and Meserve's Purchase, and the part of the railway system nearest the summit was in Sargent's Purchase.

The heights of the Cog Railway are as follows:

Climbing the White Mountains of New Hampshire

Base Station	2,565 feet
Waumbac Tank	3,910 feet
Jacob's Ladder	4,835 feet
Gulf Tank	5,638 feet
Summit	6,288 feet

Nearly half a mile of the road was built before any sawed lumber was used in its construction. Further completion of the road was rushed with all possible speed, and in July 1869, the first train reached the summit.

The entire length of the cog road is three and a quarter miles. This trestle form of construction greatly reduced the work of grading and also lengthened the life of the supporting woodwork.

On Jacob's Ladder, the steepest portion, the grade on the line is 37.41 percent, or a vertical rise of about four feet for every ten feet on the horizon. The average grade of this road is 1,300 feet to the mile, but occasionally this increases to nearly 2,000 feet to the mile or sinks to about 800 feet. There are nine curves in the line, varying from a 497- to 945-foot radius. Water was taken from tanks located at proper distances on the route. During the trip of three and a quarter miles, the train ascends 3,700 feet per mile. The roadbed follows the path nearly all the way as it was originally laid out by Ethan Allen Crawford in 1821 and improved into a bridle path soon after by Horace Fabyan.

The ascent of the cog begins at the Marshfield House base station at an elevation of approximately 2,700 feet above sea level. The summit of the mountain has an elevation of 6,288 feet.

This is considered the second steepest rack railway in the world, with an average grade of over 25 percent and a maximum grade of 37.41 percent. The railway ascends the mountain at 2.8 miles per hour and descends at 4.6 miles per hour; however, the new biodiesel locomotives can ascend in approximately thirty-seven minutes. Total round trip is sixty-five minutes up and forty minutes to descend. The length of the track is approximately 3.0 miles.

Originally, it was stated that the Cog Railway was a narrow-gauge railway. The book *Mt. Washington in Winter: 1870–71*, published in 1871, refers to the gauge as four feet, seven inches in width. The booklet *The Mt. Washington Cog Railway*, published by the Mt. Washington Railway Company in 1966, refers to the gauge as being four feet, eight inches. Accordingly, the gauge is most nearly that of the American Standard Gauge (four feet, eight and a half inches). This slight variation in width reasonably occurs due to temperature changes and other factors on the mountain.

With the completion of the Cog Railway and the increased tourist business via the Boston, Concord & Montreal and later, in 1895, the Boston & Maine Railroad, Mr. Walter Aiken began to play a more prominent role in the operation of the railway. (Walter was one of the sons of Herrick Aiken.)

Now the demand to build more locomotives was apparent for the Railway Company. They were built in Walter Aiken's shop; thus, he became more prominent in the affairs of the company. According to Glen M. Kidder, Mr. Aiken accepted stock in the railway in payment for the locomotives. Later, Mr. Aiken, now the general manager of the railway, was elected president of the company in 1886. (See Appendix B, "Chronological List of Locomotives.")

Glen M. Kidder's *Railway to the Moon* notes:

> *In 1874 the first of the horizontal-boiler locomotives appeared by the Manchester Locomotive Works on Manchester, New Hampshire, and having one pair of cylinders for each axle. This locomotive No. 3, "Hercules" and the later ones, were distinctive because of their appearance. The boiler and smoke box tilted forward so that the front was about 18-inches lower than the back of the boiler, thus striking a compromise between the position of being on level terrain or being on a steep grade. This enabled the locomotive to steam much better and to perform more uniformly. The tender was on a separate chassis and was attached to the rear of the engine.*
>
> *During the next 34 years a total of nine more locomotives (including the two built originally for the Green Mt. [Maine] Railway) were built by the Manchester Locomotive Works, or its successor, Alco-Manchester Locomotive Works. The Railway's present locomotives follow more or less the same general design, although the cab design has changed quite a little over the years.*

MAJOR CHANGES IN LEADERSHIP OF THE COMPANY

Sylvester Marsh slowly faded into an advisory position, and as time passed he moved to Concord, New Hampshire, where, on December 30, 1884, he passed away. After his death, control of the Cog Railway was passed to the Concord & Montreal Railroad, which ran it until 1895, when the Boston & Maine took control.

Glen M. Kidder's account continues:

> *As a result of Walter Aiken's death in 1893 after which the Concord and Montreal Railroad bought up his stock holdings in the Mt. Washington*

Climbing the White Mountains of New Hampshire

Railway, the latter was controlled almost entirely by the Concord and Montreal Railroad. However, this railroad soon came into the hands of the Boston and Maine Railroad, thus bringing to an end another era. By this time, however, most of those who had been closely associated with the Mt. Washington Railway from its early days no longer were around.

The Boston & Maine was in a state of change and was looking for a buyer of the railway. They were in the process of curtailing operations by eliminating the Fabyan branch line to the base of Mount Washington. At this time, the name of Henry Teague was suggested to the Boston & Maine Railroad officials, and they persuaded Mr. Teague to buy the railway for the sum of $100,000.

Mr. Teague had no previous railroad experience, but he did have good "business sense." In 1931, he bought the Cog Railway from the Boston & Maine Railroad. The colonel, as he was known, soon made changes and promoted the railway vigorously as a tourist attraction. He increased the number of daily trips and reduced the fares in order to attract more passengers.

Colonel Teague soon began to show a profit despite the Great Depression and the fall of the stock market. He instituted a unique profit-sharing plan among his employees; thus, most of his help returned for many years to come.

On September 21, 1938, the greatest hurricane ever to strike New England caused extensive damage throughout the White Mountains and the Cog Railway. About a half mile of Jacob's Ladder trestle was completely destroyed. It was soon repaired, at a cost of $60,000, and opened for business that fall.

During the Depression years, the colonel met up with Arthur S. Teague (no relation), the colonel's right-hand man, who took a strong interest in the railway. Over the years with the railway, he developed a turnout system at appropriate locations on the railway. In 1941, a nine-motion switch was invented so the cars and cog engines could pass and repass one another. The two spur sidings were added, each long enough to divert two upward traveling trains so another could pass down, enabling more round trips per day.

In 2004, work was completed replacing the lower Waumbet Switch and Siding with an eighteen-hundred-foot pass loop equipped with electric- and hydraulic-powered automated switches. These switches are powered by batteries and recharged by solar panels. One switch is located at each end of the loop, allowing ascending and descending trains to pass one another.

Upon Colonel Teague's death on October 2, 1951, he left his estate to his alma mater, Dartmouth College. The era of Colonel Henry Teague came to a close, and Dartmouth College became the Cog Railway's new owner.

With the transfer of ownership of the railway, its future was up in the air. It would be difficult to replace the leadership and business experience of Colonel Henry Teague. However, the late colonel's right-hand man, Arthur S. Teague, was available to take the helm. Mr. Teague became the general manager. During his tenure, Arthur S. Teague made additional improvements to the Cog Railway, such as the improvement of the machine shop with new modern equipment.

In November 1962, trustees of Dartmouth College decided to sell the Mount Washington properties, their real estate and the building at the base to the Railway Corporation headed by Arthur Teague.

Later, in 1964, the State of New Hampshire acquired the summit of Mount Washington from Dartmouth College and leased the Summit House to the Cog Railway.

After Arthur Teague's death in 1967, ownership was passed on to his wife, Ellen C. Teague, who operated the railway until there were some difficulties with the state's Public Utilities Commission and she was forced to close in 1981. The Public Utilities Commission refused to allow operation of the railway while track maintenance and rebuilding was done. In 1983, Ellen Teague sold the railway to a group of New Hampshire businessmen.

In 2008, the Presby and Bedor families celebrated twenty-five years as owners of the Mount Washington Cog Railway. Today, under the leadership of Joel and Cathy Bedor and partner Wayne Presby, general manager Bob Clement and Mike Kenly, shop foreman, along with their dedicated crew, have restored all six coal-fired locomotives, built a new base station, replaced tracks, improved the switching system and made many improvements to the grounds. Also in 2008, new biodiesel locomotives were introduced into the line of locomotives.

5

OLD PEPPERSASS

The first locomotive ever to be built on the Cog Railway was named Hero and later Peppersass because of its vertical boiler, which resembles to a pepper sauce bottle. In those days, all locomotives were named and bore such names as Cloud, Atlas and George Stephenson.

Although Old Peppersass was a complete success in every way, being in regular use for twelve years on the cog road, various improvements gradually suggested themselves, with the result that the next engines were made considerably different in various details.

Guy Roberts and Frank H. Burt provided some of the following accounts of Old Peppersass in their 1930 publication *Old Peppersass*:

The upright boiler was retained but with a different style of smokestack and without swinging features. An enclosed cab was provided and an improved type of tender adopted. In Old Peppersass the cylinders worked forward to the small cog-wheels in front of the boiler, while in the later type the action was toward the rear, with a much larger cog-wheel placed under the cab, with better speed resulting. Mr. Walter Aiken, a mechanic and manager of the Cog Railway, was most helpful in developing this improvement type of engine.

The original engine was built by Campbell & Whittier of Boston, and was used until it became worn out. It was exhibited at the World's Fair in Chicago in 1893 and at the Buffalo Fair in 1906, since which time it had been in the keeping of the Baltimore & Ohio Railroad, at Baltimore, Maryland, and was a part of the "Iron Horse Fair," promoted by this company and held in 1928.

This locomotive was later found after being lost for many years, as it had been transported to many parts of the country for exhibitions. The Reverend Guy Roberts, pastor of the Methodist Episcopal Church in Whitefield, New Hampshire, who in 1916 was noted for saving the profile of the Old Man of the Mountain in Franconia Notch and is the author of a series of booklets describing the White Mountains, took the initiative in finding Old Peppersass and getting it back into New Hampshire and to its former owner.

After much correspondence trying to locate the old engine and conferences with Colonel W.A. Barron of the Crawford House, Roberts turned the matter over to the officials of the Boston & Maine Railroad, who have since brought about Old Peppersass's return, repair and permanent housing at the Bretton Woods station in front of the Mount Pleasant House near Mount Washington.

The Boston & Maine Railroad decided to restore Old Peppersass and make a commemorative trip for the railway's sixtieth anniversary. In order that due observance might be made of the return of this original mountain-climbing locomotive to its Mount Washington home, and in order to make New Hampshire's recreational attraction even more widely known, Boston & Maine Railroad officials, acting in conjunction with the State of New Hampshire Publicity Bureau and other interested citizens, arranged for a Gala Day on July 20, 1929, when Old Peppersass was formerly restored to the scenes that had made it famous. On June 26, 1929, Old Peppersass was actually returned to the base and was thoroughly tried out during the following weeks prior to the Gala Day occasion.

A CELEBRATION

On July 20, 1929, the Reverend Guy Roberts was present to join in the gala celebration of the return of Old Peppersass. His personal rendering is as follows:

This day, a Saturday, the weather was perfect, pleasant, warm, and without wind. Elaborate preparations were made for the event. A temporary grandstand had been erected just beyond the building at the Base for the accommodation of various invited guests, and a speakers' platform was also provided. Everything was in readiness with flags and bunting. The little stationhouse was draped with a reproduction of the State seal. Motion picture cameras and reporters were present recording the events of the day.

Climbing the White Mountains of New Hampshire

Old Peppersass as seen on the day of the Gala Day celebration, July 20, 1929, its final run up the mountain.

The last of the six heavily loaded trains up the mountain, preceding Old Peppersass, drew a trailer loaded with cameramen and movie operators; these and the reporters aboard the regular passenger car duly recorded the ascent of the famous old relic as it nobly climbed the mountain again after half a century of inactivity. The Whitefield Band was present providing music in support of the event.

Governor Charles W. Tobey of New Hampshire and Governors of six other states were present. President George Hannauer and Mr. T Frank Joyce, Assist. Vice President of the Boston and Maine Railroad and other officials of the Boston and Maine Railroad were present, as were many other dignitaries. In all some 500 invitations had been issued by the Boston and Maine.

A luncheon at Mount Washington was available for the invited guests. Following, the famous old Crawford Coach, that years ago had carried hundreds of passengers into the Cog-road at the Base, now drawn by six horses and driven by George Howland from Crawfords', conveyed Governor C.W. Tobey, George Hannauer, Colonel W.A. Baron, Governor Christianson of Minnesota, Governor John E. Weeks of Vermont, Mr. Thomas N. Perkins, Chairman of the Board of Directors of the Boston and Maine Railroad, Ex-Gov. J.J. Cornwell of West Virginia, now General Counsel of the Baltimore and Ohio Railroad, and the Reverend Guy Roberts, to the special trains at Bretton Woods station which took all the guests to the Base, the two trains being heavily loaded and properly decorated. The regular trains for the day to the summit were cancelled.

Exercises at the Base took place at 2:00 on Saturday—July 20, 1929, with Colonel Barron, proprietor of the Crawford House, presiding as toastmaster. In his introductory remarks he referred to the unusualness losing a locomotive in contrast to the proverbial needle in a hay-stack, giving the previously mentioned Reverend Roberts due credit for finding the ancient engine, and instigating its return to its mountain home; he then introduced Rev. Mr. Roberts who bowed in recognition to the applause.

The Honorable J.J. Cornwell, former Governor of West Virginia, General Counsel of the Baltimore and Ohio Railroad, was introduced next. In his brief remarks he formally presented Old Peppersass to Mr. George Hannauer, President of the Boston and Maine Railroad. Mr. Hannauer responded, graciously accepting the old engine from the Baltimore and Ohio Railroad people, and in turn presenting it to Governor Charles W. Tobey, for the State of New Hampshire. Governor Tobey then accepted the gift, on behalf of the State and in the interest of the further development of the recreational interests of the State by a most fitting speech.

OLD PEPPERSASS CLIMBS AGAIN

Roberts's account continues:

At the proper moment Old Peppersass came chugging up the track from the engine house, blowing its whistle and being most enthusiastically greeted by the cheering crowd. Col. Barron had previously climbed to the Lakes of the Clouds and secured a bottle of its sparkling water, which was used at the conclusion of the speeches by Mr. Hannauer in christening Old Peppersass, dedicating it to the further development of the recreational interests of the White Mountains.

Soon, after the close of the literary part of the exercises, the six cog trains started up the mountain, loaded to capacity with the guests of the occasion, and with Old Peppersass going along last. In charge were engineer "Jack" E.C. Frost and fireman William I. Newsham, both of Concord, and also accompanied by Mr. Lawrence Richardson, Chief Mechanical Officer of the Boston and Maine Railroad.

Despite its age of 63 years, and being idle for nearly 50 years, Old Peppersass made the climb as easily as in the days of its youth, scaling the steep 36.6 per cent grade of Jacob's Ladder as vigorously as ever.

Climbing the White Mountains of New Hampshire

As all was going so well, it was decided on the way up, to go further than was first intended, to the top of Jacob's Ladder, and the entire trip to the summit could easily be made. When, within about half a mile from the top, at the reservoir of the Gulf Tank, it was decided to start back, however, on account of not longer delaying the return of the six trains waiting at the summit.

Old Peppersass easily started back and that with five persons aboard, the son of the engineer and two others having climbed aboard en-route without authority. All went well until half a mile of the return journey had been covered and the vicinity of bent number 800 [The Cog-road is built in 12-foot sections, called "bents," and these are numbered from 1 at the foot to 1,200 at the top of the mountain.] *reached, when evidently a tooth broke out of one of the gear wheels. This caused the engine to jump up at the upper, forward end, and on dropping back the cogwheel came down at the right hand side of the cog-rail and of course not in mesh with it.*

Instantly, the old engine began to gather speed as the pull of gravity started rushing down the steep grade of the "Long Trestle," out of control as normally afforded by the action of the engine. Frost and Newman immediately applied the hand friction brake, to the very best of their combined ability, but such speed had been gained in the few seconds interim that it was impossible to check its wild rush even in the least, and the terrible consciousness that Old Peppersass was running away and utterly beyond human control, flashed over the five men aboard the engine! Engineer Frost shouted to all to "Jump"—his son, Caleb, being the first to do so, and that without injury. Mr. D.H. Pote, of Swampscott, Massachusetts, a photographer, jumped next. Last of all, Newman and Frost jumped off. Frost himself alighted on the lower side of the track somewhere near bent number 730. Daniel P. Rossiter, official reporter and photographer for the State Publicity Bureau and the Boston and Maine for the occasion, was still aboard but was hidden from Frost by the tender as Mr. Rossiter hung from the outside of it. The engineer, fireman, and Mr. Pote received broken bones in landing, but from this they recovered in due time. Mr. Rossiter remained on, for some unknown reason, for at least 1,572 feet before dropping off, when he crashed to instant death on the jagged rocks at the bottom of Jacob's Ladder, at the foot of bend number 669. Why he did not drop off before will never be known, though it is possible that he was delayed by trying to save his camera outfit.

Old Peppersass continued its wild rush down over Jacob's Ladder, shrieking out its swan song and tearing its way down to destruction as it leaped from the track at the foot of the Ladder near the reverse curve at the bend of number 640, landing opposite bend 625 in the edge of Burts' Ravine—covering about 2,100 feet in its wild rush to death. The boiler finally stopped its flight over 100 feet from the track down in the larger growth, while the bottom of the ash pan landed near the track opposite bend number 560, a distance of 960 feet from where the engine left the rails. Just how it got there is not known, but probably by sliding on the track and then bounding off into the brush.

While Old Peppersass wrecked itself in its final plunge, the boiler did not explode and was later recovered nearby. Reverend Guy Roberts, who stood near the upper end of Jacob's Ladder as the old engine traveled past him, hurried down the track immediately after the final crash of Old Peppersass and was the first to reach the broken and bleeding body of his friend Mr. Rossiter, arriving within five minutes after Rossiter's death. Rossiter was later taken to his young widow's home at Ludlow, Vermont, where burial occurred. The funeral was largely attended by the many friends of this popular and capable young man.

The Boston & Maine spared no expense to relieve the tragedy of the twentieth of its disastrous consequences to the fullest possible extent. The

Four trains are seen leaving the base station for the ascent to the summit of Mount Washington.

remains of Old Peppersass were resurrected from its Burt's Ravine grave and taken to the repair shop at Concord, New Hampshire, where the old engine was fully repaired and restored during the following winter. Early in the season of 1930, it was taken back again to its mountain home and placed on permanent display at the Bretton Woods station in front of the Mount Pleasant House, in keeping with earlier intention, where this priceless old relic may easily be seen by all.

Since that time, there have been no more experiments with relics of the past. Old Peppersass is presently on exhibit near the base station.

There was a second accident on September 17, 1967, which the Mount Washington Cog Railway has published as follows:

> *There were eight passengers killed and seventy-two injured when Engine No. 3 derailed at the skyline switch about a mile below the summit. The engine rolled off the trestle while the uncoupled passenger car slid several hundred feet into a large rock. An investigation revealed that the Skyline switch had not been properly configured for the descending train. The railway nonetheless has a solid safety record, having taken almost five million people to the summit during its existence.*

6

The Marshfield House

The Turnpike and Railroad Extension

In connection with building the cog road, a turnpike was built from the Fabyan House to the base, a distance of six miles. This was completed in 1869 and afforded vehicle access to the cog road.

The White Mountain Railroad, having reached Fabyan's in 1874, was extended from there to the beginning of the cog road and opened to traffic in July 1876. This local extension did away with the service over the toll road, or turnpike, leading to the cog road, which it had served during the preceding five years. Later, this road was turned over to the state and is today used by automobiles to reach the base and the Marshfield Station, as well as the auto parking grounds.

In 1895, the Boston & Maine leased the line connection from the base station with Fabyan's station. The wild plain, which occupied nearly the entire basin formed by the mountains surrounding the locality, was certainly not without peculiar attractions of its own during the summer months. The dark shading of the foliage of its coniferous growth, the suggestiveness of its mysterious depths and its overshadowing by the grand elevation all around lend an almost supernatural quality not wholly uninviting.

The Base Station

When the cog road was first built, it ended about a quarter of a mile nearer the Ammonoosuc River at the foot of the mountain than it does now. The

The original Old Peppersass is on display at the Marshfield base station, September 23, 2010.

base station buildings were grouped together in a motley fashion, with no thought of the artistic. Here were found stagecoach barns, a machine shop and an ungainly three-story depot with a small waiting room and bedrooms above for railway employees. There was also the old Marshfield House.

THE OLD MARSHFIELD HOUSE

From 1871 to 1895, there existed as part of the previously described original base station group a two-and-a-half-story hotel called the Marshfield House.

It is not known who built the Marshfield House, although the proprietor in 1873 was E.K. Cox. Three large barns were connected with it for the use of stage drivers before the railroad was extended from Fabyan's to the base, and these were often filled to capacity. The name Marshfield House was given because the locality of the base station had been known in the early years of the enterprise as Marshfield, in honor of Sylvester Marsh, the inventor of the cog road. How this name has come back in a changed form will be related later in the chapter.

In the spring of 1895, all the buildings, with the exception of the Marshfield House, were burned. This afforded an opportunity to rebuild nearer the junction of the cog road and the branch from Fabyan's, with the present more pleasing structure at the base station of the mountain located twenty-seven hundred feet above sea level. With the completion of the next base station boardinghouse, the older house was deserted and soon became a source of danger from tramp occupancy. Removable parts of value and furnishings were taken out, and the rest of the remaining structure was burned, thus ending its existence. Following Mr. Cox as proprietor of the Marshfield House came David Aldrich of Whitefield, George Crawford of Bristol and Edwin Judkins and Harrison Davis of Franklin, New Hampshire. Today, at the new base station, we may browse through a gift shop, eat at the restaurant, visit the informative museum and enjoy the magnificent views before ascending the mountain.

REMINISCE ABOUT THE OLD MARSHFIELD HOUSE

The old-timers will tell you that years ago there could be found around the big stove in the Marshfield House almost any summer evening—for at this elevation heat was often needed even in the summertime— such men as John Horne of Lakeport, New Hampshire, who was regularly employed by the Mt. Washington Railway Company from 1873 to his retirement many years ago and who for many years was a most efficient superintendent of the

Two Cog Railway workers descend Mount Washington via the sliding boards, July 1929.

cog road; Ed Judkins, conductor of the road, full bearded and reserved; Sam Butterworth, engineer and machinist; Uncle John Camden, road master, with service dating back to 1874; Fred O. Nourse, telegraph operator of Littleton; and Walter Aiken, manufacturer, machinist, inventor and to whose ingenuity and perseverance was due the perfecting of Mr. Marsh's inventions and their application to the mountain-climbing feat. Aiken also supervised the building of the cog road, invested largely in the enterprise and, in many ways, rendered most valuable service.

Mention should also be made of Myron P. Browley, the happy-go-lucky genial conductor of the road from 1899 to 1911, whose pleasantry was as contagious as the mountain air is exhilarating; Ms. Clarke, who for some fifteen consecutive years was the dominating personality on Mount Washington for management of the Summit House in a way that made her beloved and famous as a hostess of most unusual ability; and lastly, Patrick Camden, the son of Uncle John and his successor for many years as the road master of the cog road, who more than once made the descent by slide board in three minutes' time and in whose memory the Camden refuge house was built.

The Slide Boards (Devil's Shingle)

The slide board—or "devil's shingle," as it was sometimes called—on which the mountain railway employees, and at times certain others, slid down the mountain, were devised of wood and metal about three feet long and one foot wide, so arranged as to fit onto the cog rail, down which it slid in toboggan-like fashion, its speed being controlled by lifting up on the friction brake handles on either side. No two boards were alike. They were approximately ninety-five inches in length and nine and four-fifths inches wide.

On several occasions, the summit-published daily paper, *Among the Clouds*, was sent down the mountain in this way as a "newspaper train" in the early morning so it might reach its off-the-mountain readers during their breakfast hour. The record slide from the summit to the Ammonoosuc River, a distance of three miles, is recorded at two minutes and forty-five seconds. By 1906, the slide board was finally forbidden by the operating railroad company after the accidental death of an employee and a serious accident to another while sliding down the mountain. Later, the design of the track was changed so the old braking mechanism could not grip any more.

Track inspector Patrick Camden, road master of the cog road, rides the slide board on the Cog Railway, 1929.

An essential feature of the Cog Railway was the driving mechanical board. On the track, in addition to the outside rail, is a central cog rail consisting of two pieces of wrought-angle iron, placed parallel and connected by iron pins four inches apart. The teeth on the driving wheel mesh with the cog rail.

THE MARSHFIELD STATION

When the automobile came into constant use during the mid-twenty-first century, travel to the base greatly increased because of its novelty and the wondrous wooded beauty of the countryside across its entire distance of six miles from Fabyan's to Bretton Woods. At first, cars were packed by the base station boardinghouse while their occupants ascended the mountain by rail or on foot. In 1925, the road was extended to a point near the site of the Old Marshfield House, and a clearing was made, providing ample parking space. Many tourists have been known to hike up the mountain near the tracks; the climb, however, is most strenuous, requiring about three hours' time for a seasoned climber. None others should attempt it.

The Marshfield House and the Mount Washington Cog Railway are located on the west side of the mountain at the base station, 1950s.

7

Ascent of Mount Washington
via the "Cog"

The ascent of the Mount Washington Cog Railway can be achieved with perfect assurance and 100 percent safety, as mentioned earlier. The trip should be made in order to appreciate the views during the excursion up the mountain, as no description can do justice to their magnificence.

In order to do them justice in our ascent up the mountain, let us return to the mid-1880s, when skeptical but adventurous tourists would celebrate the beauty, romance and mystery of the White Mountains. The following is a narrative of our journey to the summit of Mount Washington, which I have transcribed from several past reminisces:

My friends and I are at the base station and observe the strange-looking engine. The question now is: how much power is necessary to overcome gravity and lift the weight of the machine into the air? Mr. Sylvester Marsh has not precisely lifted the mountain, but he has, nevertheless, with the aid of Mr. Walter Aiken, reduced it, to all intents, to a level.

It appeared that everything was knocked out of place. But this queer-looking machine, with bulldog tenacity, literally hung on to the mountain with its teeth. It, however, was capable of performing a feat such as Watt never dreamed of, or Stephenson imagined. It went up the mountain as easily as a bear climbed a tree.

I had observed the last ascent of the train, which usually reached the summit at sunset, and I had pleased myself with considering whether it most resembled a big, shining beetle crawling up the mountainside or some fiery dragon dragging his prey after him to his den, after ravaging the valley.

Now it was our turn. It was a cold afternoon in September when we entered the little car, not much larger than a streetcar, and felt the premonitory jerk with which the ascent began. The first hill was so steep that one would look up to see the track always mountain

Climbing the White Mountains of New Hampshire

The crew of the Cog waits at the base station with the engineer to ascend Mount Washington.

high above the head. We soon got used to the novelty, and to the clatter which accompanied the incessant dropping of a pawl into the indentures of the cogged rails, and in which we recognized an element of safety. It seemed that the train did not move faster than we could walk, but it moved steadily, except when it now and then stopped at the water tank, standing solitary and alone upon the waste of rocks.

By the time we emerged above the timber line into the chill and wind-swept desolation above it—a first sight of which was so amazing—the sun had set behind the Green Mountains, showing a long, serrated line of crimson peaks, above which clouds of lake floated in a sea of amber. I grew very cold. Jackets and shawls were quickly put on. From here we passed the small Halfway shelter hut, and we were slowly approaching Jacob's Ladder.

The steepest pitch in this railway was found here at Jacob's Ladder, where the grade was thirteen and one-quarter inches to every 3 feet, or 36.6 percent. At this point, the trestle crossed a ravine at a height of 20 feet, the Ladder itself being about 325 feet long, the elevation here being approximately 4,751 feet. The view was breathtaking. The colors on the surrounding mountains were brilliant. On the right during our ascent was the Ammonoosuc Ravine; however, on the left was the spectacular depth of the Burt Ravine a thousand feet below, named in honor of the late Henry M. Burt, founder and publisher of the newspaper Among the Clouds. *Searching northeast up the Presidential was Mount Jefferson in the distance. While no angels ascend or descend over it to a sleeping son of*

Jacob's Ladder is a massive trestle over which the cogwheel engine pushes the coach up the steep side of Mount Washington. Jacob's Ladder received its name from the famed Ethan Allen Crawford as his trail up the mountain traversed this area, noted for its steepness and where one's mountain climbing abilities are subjected to severe test. The steepest grade at this point is 37.4 percent—a vertical rise of about four feet for every ten feet on the horizontal. August 1920.

Israel at its foot, and while its top does not reach into the heavens, it does reach into the region of arctic vegetation and life, as is later referred.

Leaving Jacob's Ladder, the tree line was soon passed, and we entered the region of subarctic and arctic vegetation and insects, of which there could be found some 125 species of the former and hundreds of the latter, and such as are found nowhere else nearer than Labrador. Presently, we arrived into actual touch of an arctic climate by a trip of a little over two miles up this unique railway.

*The next stop was at the Gulf Tank, where the engine again quenched it thirst. While doing so the passengers could step out to a brink of the Great Gulf into which the precipitous side of Mount Clay descends for nearly two thousand feet, with Spaulding Lake far below, this named in remembrance of John H. Spaulding. The delicate little white blossoms of the Greenland Sandwort (*Arennaria greenlandica)*, a true arctic flower, could be found round about during early summer. The mountain peaks seen at the left were Mounts Clay, Jefferson, Adams and Madison.*

Resuming our journey, the ruined walls of one of Crawford's stone cabins could be seen at the right. The Carriage (Auto) Road coming up at the left was soon upon us, with Lizzie Bourne's monument at the right of the tracks. Up the engine toiled and panted, while we watched the valleys, streams and mountains pass. The lights from the

Summit House seemed a welcoming sight. It was now but a few rods to the Summit House, where ends the most remarkable view of the world below and of the various peaks near and far. Stiffened with cold, we rushed for the open door without ceremony. In an instant, the car was empty, while the engine, dripping with unheard-of efforts, seemed to regard this desertion with reproachful glances. This was the termination point of our fantastic excursion to the summit of Mount Washington.

Near the top of Mount Washington, close by the railroad track, there is a pile of rocks that passing travelers have heaped on the spot where Lizzie Bourne perished. Ms. Bourne ascended the mountain in the summer of 1855. Her party set out in the afternoon from the Glen House and was overtaken near the summit by clouds that hid the summit from view. Overcome by the terrific winds, which swept the rocky summit, Lizzie sank, fainting and exhausted, and died in the arms of her uncle. The survivors wrapped her body in their coats and kept a vigil through the long and weary night. In the morning, they discovered with amazement how near the summit they were.

At the summit, there are many attractions besides the magnificent vistas that surround the Presidential Range, such as the spacious Sherman Adams Summit Building with its gift shop and snack bar; the historic Tip-Top House; the Mount Washington Observatory; and the Summit Museum. Needless to say, the views are spectacular, and on a clear day they may extend all the way to the Atlantic Ocean.

The Summit House as seen from the Lizzie Bourne Monument.

8

Buildings on the Summit

The first house of any sort to be built at the summit was a small stone cabin, followed immediately by two others. Ethan A. Crawford completed the building in July 1823. One of these contained a roll of sheet lead, on which the names of visitors were scratched. This was, in fact, the first "register" of Mount Washington. Owing to excessive dampness, these cabins were rarely used and finally fell into disrepair. They eventually disappeared from the summit. The ruined stonewalls of one of these huts may still be seen near the tank by the Cog Railway.

The First Summit House

Following the abandoning of Crawford's stone cabin, a large tent was erected near the summit, enclosing a sheet-iron stove. This soon proved impractical because of the violent weather that so often occurred on the summit. Next came a rude wooden shelter approximately twelve square feet, which gave some protection.

Following these crude attempts for shelter on the summit came the building's first hotel. This was fittingly named the Summit House and was built on the north side of the peak in 1852–53 by J.S. Hall, Lucius M. Rosebrook of Lancaster and Nathan R. Perkins of Jefferson. This structure was constructed of heavy stone taken from the mountaintop; it was twenty-four by sixty-four feet in size and was firmly secured in place by

The Tip-Top House was the oldest structure standing on the summit of Mount Washington. Erected in 1853, the house had sheltered world-famous men. The Tip-Top survived the summit fire of 1908; however, it was destroyed by fire in 1915. It was restored in 1916 with the addition of a covered stone passageway connecting it to the Summit House.

cement, heavy bolts and four strong cables over the flat roof. Lumber had to be brought up two or three sticks at a time on horseback. Mr. Rosebrook carried the heavy front door up the mountain from the Glen House on his back before the Carriage (Auto) Road was built.

In 1853, this house was enlarged, and an upper floor with a pitched roof was added. Withstanding the storms for over thirty years, it was used as the headquarters for the hotel help after the second Summit House was built, finally being demolished in 1884.

THE FIRST TIP-TOP HOUSE

In 1853, the Tip-Top House was erected to compete with the Summit House. The house, built at a cost of $7,000 by Samuel F. Spaulding & Company, was made of rough stone blasted from the summit of the mountain. It measured twenty-eight by eighty-four feet in size. A deck roof was constructed on which visitors might stand to secure an unobstructed view, which was also enhanced by the use of a telescope, weather permitting. A few cows were once kept for the benefit of this hotel and were pastured near the seventh post on the Carriage Road, on a grassy plateau since called the Cow Pasture.

The next year, the Summit House was sold to the Spauldings, who conducted the two hotels as one for nine years. They were followed by Colonel John R. Hitchcock of Gorham until 1872. Hitchcock added a pitched-roof story to the Tip-Top House, in which seventeen little bedrooms were provided. When the newspaper *Among the Clouds* moved to a new location, the Tip-Top House was abandoned and fell into disrepair.

A three-story, ninety-one-room hotel was built on top of Mount Washington together with a weather observatory. All these building were destroyed in the fire of 1908 except the Tip-Top House, which was renovated to again function as a hotel. When the Summit House was replaced, however, the Tip-Top House burned. It was rebuilt as an annex to the Summit House and was then abandoned in 1968. Now a state historic site, the Tip-Top was restored in 1987, including its flat roof. Today, the structure is surrounded by other buildings and a parking lot. In 1982, the Tip-Top House was added to the National Register of Historic Places.

THE SECOND SUMMIT HOUSE

Following the completion of the cog road to the summit, steps were taken to provide a new Summit House in 1872–73. This action was financed by Walter Aiken, manager of the Mount Washington Railway Company, and President John E. Lyon of the Boston, Concord & Montreal Railroad. The Summit House opened to the public in July 1873. It had accommodations for 150 guests; was thoroughly built, consuming 250 trainloads of material costing over $60,000; and served well its purpose for thirty-five seasons, at last to be destroyed in the great fire of June 18, 1908. The hotel was the focal point of interest and received a host of visitors annually.

The successive proprietors of this second Summit House were Captain John W. Dodge; his widow, Harriet D. Dodge; Charles G. Emmons; and, from 1886 until it was destroyed by fire, the Barron, Merrill and Barron Company, with Ms. Mattie A. Clarke as manager for most of that period.

Following the burning of this Summit House, the old Tip-Top House, which the flames had spared, was restored and used again after an interval of thirty-five years of disuse, as the only hotel on the summit. It remained such for a period of seven years.

The Summit House on the summit of Mount Washington. It was built to replace the old Summit House.

THE THIRD SUMMIT HOUSE

Within a few years after the burning of all the summit buildings in 1908, except the old Tip-Top House, plans were announced and surveys made for building a Summit House that would have been most outstanding. This was to have been a massive circular house of stone, concrete, steel and glass, with the very peak of the mountain showing in the center of the house. On top of the house, there was to be a mighty searchlight whose flashing rays could be seen for hundreds of miles around. A scenic electric railroad without cogs, with about a 6 percent grade, twenty miles in length and encircling the summit one-half time, was to run on the present famous and well-proven cog road. Because of various economic conditions, however, this elaborate plan, which would have cost some $1.5 million, was abandoned, and a more practical, though less spectacular, plan was adopted whereby the present simple character of the summit was retained.

An extended article titled "The Trolley on the Presidential" elaborates the plans for the railroad and house on top of Mount Washington (see chapter ten).

A NEW HOUSE ON THE SUMMIT

A new house was opened to the public on August 21, 1915. This was the most substantially built house, thoroughly anchored to the summit rocks, 168 feet long and 38 feet wide, one and a half stories high and comfortable in all it provisions, with steam heat, hot and cold water, bathrooms and lavatories, a huge fireplace, electric lights, telephone connections and the purest of mountain spring water. Under the proprietorship of the Barron Merrill, with Mr. A.D. Wright as manager, it well answered the needs of the guests. In the upper floors of the building there were twenty-two guest rooms accommodating ninety guests, a writing and lounging room, toilets and an excellent restaurant to meet the needs of all, regardless of the weather, during the summit vacation. A large bell over the entrance announced the departure of the trains and also awakened the sleeping guests on mornings that afforded a fine sunrise. It is recorded that the day on the summit is about forty minutes longer than off the mountain.

Today, the two principal public buildings on the summit are the Tip-Top House and the Sherman Adams Summit Building, both of which are owned by the State of New Hampshire and operated by the Mount Washington State Park.

The Sherman Adams Summit Building serves as the headquarters of the Mount Washington State Park. It is a large, reinforced concrete building, built into the summit's north slope. On a clear day, its windows provide a fine view toward the Northern Presidential Range. It was opened in 1980.

The Adams Building features a cafeteria and gift shop. A park rangers' station can assist visitors and offers restrooms and a post office, which is operated by the staff of the Cog Railway. The lower level of the building features the Mount Washington Summit Museum with exhibits on weather and local flora and fauna. The building was dedicated to Sherman Adams, one of New Hampshire's former governors and prominent statesman. A hikers' pack room is also provided in the Adams Building, where hikers may haul their packs and take a break before continuing their treks. Unlike at the Summit Hotel, there are no public provisions for overnight accommodations in the building. Camping is not allowed anywhere in the fifty-nine-acre Mount Washington Park.

The Sherman Adams Building is also the site of the Mount Washington Observatory. The observatory is a private, nonprofit, member-supported organization, which is involved in environmental monitoring, including weather observation, and specializes in scientific research, testing and education. The observatory moved into the Sherman Adams Building in 1980.

THE MOUNT WASHINGTON OBSERVATORY

Various old summit pictures show an observatory of one style or another on the summit's peak. The original weather observatory was built by Timothy Estus of Jefferson, New Hampshire. It was an open framework forty feet high and had a crude elevator, worked by hand with crank and gearing, with a lifting capacity of eight persons. Although it cost $600, it was abandoned as a failure after a few months' use and was torn down in 1856.

The first regular meteorological observation on Mount Washington was conducted by the United States Signal Service from 1870 to 1892, a precursor of the Weather Bureau. The Mount Washington station was the first of its kind in the world and set an example for other countries.

The federal government inaugurated a weather bureau service on the summit in May 1871, fitting up a room in the barnlike train shed for headquarters. This room was used until 1874, when a low, staunch and firmly braced wooden building called the Signal Station was built for this use. The establishment of this service by the government followed a winter's volunteer service organized by Professor Charles H. Hitchcock of Dartmouth College, with J.H. Huntington in charge of the work and with S.A. Nelson, A.F. Clough, H.A. Kimball and Sergeant Theodore Smith assisting. Nelson and Smith spent the entire winter on the summit. Clough and Kimball were photographers for the project.

The federal government assisted during this one year by furnishing weather-observing apparatus, the telegraph wire and outfits and Sergeant Smith as observer. The weather records made here were the first continuous records taken in both summer and winter on any mountain in America. Thrilling stories of weather phenomena were telegraphed far and wide, and the country in general read the details of weather extremes, sensational experiences and sufferings rarely equaled except in the older Polar expeditions.

The government continued its Signal Service work here during the summer and winter until 1887, and then only in the summer for the next five years. Heroic tales of faithful endurance and suffering fill the records of these seventeen years. William Stevens died in service on the summit in February 1872. From 1878 to 1880, Sergeant Winfield Scott Jewell was sent here by the government, at his own request, to take charge of the preparation for the Greeley Arctic expedition. (Jewell perished on the Greeley Arctic expedition.)

At times in the Signal Station, the hottest of fires in two stoves in the small room could not keep water from freezing three feet away. Many times, butter had to be cut with a chisel and hammer, while salt pork was sawed off like a stick of wood. The lowest temperature recorded by the Signal Service was fifty-nine degrees below zero, while the highest wind velocity at the time was 186 miles per hour, the highest on record at that time. As noted later in this chapter, that record was broken in April 1934.

The second observatory was built in 1880 by the Mount Washington Railway Company. This was twenty-seven feet high, of a pyramidal shape and became a favorite lookout. In 1892, it was made another story higher, and for that reason a powerful searchlight was operated from it. For the first few summers after its erection, the tower was used by the United States Coast and Geodetic Survey in its work, but later, in 1902, it fell into disrepair and was finally taken down. It had no successor.

The Mount Washington Observatory reoccupied the summit in 1932 through the enthusiasm of a group of individuals who recognized the importance of a scientific facility. The present observatory was launched in that year with a grant from the New Hampshire Academy of Science, and the first scientists from around the world gathered their meteorological observations to help develop new theories about weather. In April 1934, the observatory measured a wind gust of 231 miles per hour, which remains the world record for a surface station. The relationship with the U.S. Weather Service has always been close, but the observatory is not a part of any government agency.

The observatory continues to record weather information. It also serves as an important station for the measurement of cosmic ray activity in the upper atmosphere. The Mount Washington Observatory is considered the only station to have remained in continuous operation with an ever-extending mission.

In addition to its meteorological work, the observatory maintains a natural laboratory research facility for the study of most aspects of icing, cloud and atmospheric phenomena and for the testing of instruments, devices and materials.

In addition to the observatory, the Mount Washington Museum has offered a first-class educational service since 1973. All the exhibits have been prepared by the observatory staff with the assistance and advice of museum professionals and authorities in history, geology, biology, etc. The Mount Washington Museum has drawn on a large collection of White Mountain books, photographs and further artifacts located at the observatory's Educational Resource Center in North Conway. This center was established in 1991 and invites the public to visit it for information concerning membership, audiovisual presentations, publications and other educational programs.

This is an aerial view of the weather installation on the Mount Washington Observatory in the winter. The observatory is considered a Class-A weather station for the U.S. Weather Bureau.

OUTBUILDINGS ON THE SUMMIT

Three train sheds have appeared and disappeared on the summit. The first one, a combined station and train house built in 1870 and located in front of the site of the Summit House (the Sherman Adams Building), was blown down in the great storm of January 1877. A second shed, built west of the Summit House, was torn down in July 1904, while the third shed, built in approximately 1890, was burned in the fire of 1908. At present, there is no shed, and none seems to be needed, as trains do not regularly remain at the summit overnight.

Stage Buildings

The building of the Carriage Road to the summit naturally called for stables there and also for a stage office building. The latter was built in 1878 for the accommodation of stage drivers. It also became used as sleeping quarters by hikers over the mountain trails. Two large barns for stable use were erected a bit below the summit at the end of the Carriage Road. They are no longer in existence.

AMONG THE CLOUDS NEWSPAPER

The highest flight of a newspaper enterprise in the eastern states was the project of Henry M. Burt of Springfield, Massachusetts. The first issue of *Among the Clouds* appeared on July 18, 1877. Mr. Burt published the paper for twenty-one seasons and became one of the best-known figures in the White Mountains. He was honored to receive in his office President and Mrs. Hayes, Reverend and Mrs. Henry Ward Beecher, P.T. Barnum, General Joseph Hooker, Thomas A. Edison and many other distinguished guests.

The paper was printed in the old Tip-Top House until 1884, when a new office was built near the southwest corner of the Summit House. After Henry Burt's death on March 7, 1899, the newspaper was continued by his son, Frank H. Burt of Newton, Massachusetts, until the office burned down in the fire of 1908. Reginald H. Buckler continued to publish the paper in temporary quarters at the base station for several seasons. Changing conditions have since compelled it to discontinue service. Its publication was not resumed after the one year during the First World War when the Cog Railway was idle in order to do its part toward winning the war.

Mount Washington in the Presidential Range, as viewed from Little Deception Mountain.

9

Mount Washington Ravines
and Hiking the Presidential

Mount Washington is the most prominent part of the Presidential Range in the White Mountains. It is the highest mountain peak east of the Rocky Mountains and north of the Carolinas, rising to a height of 6,288 feet above sea level. We may gaze as far as the Atlantic Ocean and as far west as Lake Champlain in Vermont.

The Presidential Range lies majestically in the heart of the White Mountains. The range runs in a double curve from northeast to southwest. From the north, Mount Madison, the three additional summits include Mount Adams, Jefferson and Clay, which sweep up to Washington's summit.

To the Native Americans, the lofty summits of the Presidential Range were observed as hallowed retreats, where it was believed that only the chosen of the Great Spirit could ascend the sacred range.

The range forms a ridgeline that is approximately twelve miles in length. The range's most remarkable feature is the extensive landscape above the tree line, considered the greatest contiguous alpine area in the country east of the Mississippi. The unusual conditions above this line have led to a fascinating landscape, very barren but decorated with low spruce and fir and a variety of alpine plants. Additionally, the range is formed mostly of gneiss and mica schist, metamorphic rocks that began as sediment in a shallow sea several hundred million years ago.

The range is very popular for hikers. During good weather, hiking the Appalachian Mountain Club (AMC) trails may allow fantastic views of the surrounding White Mountains and possibly the summits in Maine, Vermont, Quebec and even New York.

A view of the Great Gulf with the northern peaks of the Presidential Range—namely, from left to right, Mounts Jefferson, Adams and Madison—in the distance.

The Presidential Range mountain peaks started to acquire their names of American chief executives about 1784. Dr. Jeremy Belknap's *History of New Hampshire* notes that the first was named to honor George Washington, who became the nation's first president in 1789. The other major summits remained unnamed until 1820, when a group of men from Lancaster, New Hampshire, led by mountain guide Ethan Allen Crawford, climbed Mount Washington and gave names to several of the surrounding peaks. They also named Mount Franklin and Mount Pleasant at that time. The remaining peaks were named more recently.

LIST OF THE PRESIDENTIAL RANGE MOUNTAINS:

Among the range's notable summits, in order from southwest to northeast, are:

Mount Webster	after Daniel Webster
Mount Jackson	after Charles Thomas Jackson (nineteenth-century geologist)
Mount Pierce	after Franklin Pierce (formerly Mount Clinton, after DeWitt Clinton)
Mount Eisenhower	after Dwight D. Eisenhower
Mount Monroe	after James Monroe
Mount Washington	after George Washington (a general at the time of naming)
Mount Clay	after Henry Clay
Mount Jefferson	after Thomas Jefferson
Mount Samuel Adams	after Samuel Adams
Mount Adams	after John Adams
Mount Quincy Adams	after John Quincy Adams.
Mount Madison	after James Madison

Additional subsidiary summits of Mount Washington include:

Ball Crag
Nelson Crag
Boott Spur

RAVINES OF MOUNT WASHINGTON

There are four large ravines on the sides of Mount Washington, each looking as though, in some mighty upheaval of the past, great chunks of the mountain slid out to no one knows where. Mention has been made of Burt's Ravine on the western side, as well as of the Great Gulf, found at the left but farther up the mountain on its northern side.

Tuckerman's Ravine as seen from Hermit Lake, 1910. This often-mentioned ravine is famous for its snow arch, which has been known to remain as late as August and is hollowed from a spur of Mount Washington. It is a horseshoe shape (coliseum), and its outer cliff is more than one thousand feet in height. This ravine was named in honor of Dr. Edward Tuckerman, professor at Amherst College.

Huntington Ravine is found off the mountain to the left just before reaching the summit by the Cog Railway, so named in honor of Professor J.H. Huntington, an ardent explorer of the White Mountains, whose Signal Station work has already been mentioned.

The cliff overhanging Huntington Ravine bears the name of Nelson Crag, given in honor of S.A. Nelson, one of Huntington's companions in the winter spent on the mountain. Farther to the right and southeast from the top, Tuckerman's Ravine is found. This is the most important of them all, as its wildness and grandeur are unsurpassed. It is named in honor of Professor Edward Tuckerman, botanist at Amherst College. The ravine is most popular for spring skiing.

HIKING THE PRESIDENTIAL RANGE

Hiking the Presidential Range may be very challenging, as the trail crosses the entire nineteen miles of the ridge. The AMC trail crosses each major summit along the way and covers at least eighty-five hundred feet in elevation. The hike may be done in a single day's trip during the summer months. During the winter, range travelers usually take two to four days. Be cautious, for several rescues of lost, overdue or injured hikers have occurred during range travel. Do not hike alone and be well equipped.

The Mount Washington Observatory and Museum offers the following description of Mount Washington in the winter:

> *The summit is usually covered with delicate frost feathers, often to a length of two feet. Composed of fog droplets that freeze on impact, these formations of rime ice grow into the wind and transform the buildings, as well as the jumble of rocks and low vegetation, into a fantasyland of beauty, unrecognizable shapes. When fog prevails, as it does most of the time, and when visibility is further affected by snow and blowing snow to produce "white-out" conditions it is sometimes impossible to see one's feet. Winds are often in excess of 100 mph, to complicate the situation further. Under such extremes, great care must be exercised to insure that no skin is exposed to the elements, that clothing is light and heat retentive, and that special equipment, such as ice axe and crampons, are in good repair.*

THE SNOW ARCH

Tuckerman's Ravine is famous for its Falls of a Thousand Streams, Hermit Lake and the Crystal Cascade, but much more so for its remarkable Snow Arch. The majestic ravine ends in a wondrous semicircular "headwall." The entire upper end is sometimes called the Mountain Coliseum. This headwall is very precipitous and about one thousand feet high, with a trail leading over it to the summit. During the winter months, great quantities of snow accumulate at the foot of the headwall, much of which is blown in from off the surrounding cliffs and summits. The depth of this great snowdrift varies with the seasons, but it must at times be over one hundred feet deep. Protected as this snowdrift is by the high encircling cliffs, it gets little sunlight during the spring months, causing the great drift to linger much longer than the snow does in other places. With the melting of the snow on the summit above, much of it runs easterly and over the headwall in small rivulets, thus producing what may be called the Falls of a Thousand Streams. Later, the falls concentrate more into two streams, which, uniting at the foot of the headwall, gully

Mount Washington's west side with the Cog Railway track ascending the left side of the mountain. Located in the center is the Ammonoosuc Ravine.

out underneath this heavily packed mass of snow, thus producing the Snow Arch. The arch, while not a glacier, is "the lifeless ghost of one." Contrary to popular opinion, snow rarely lasts here year round—1926 was the one exception—though it almost always remains throughout June into July and sometimes through August and into September.

LAKES OF THE CLOUDS

Looking down from the summit in a southwesterly direction, we see a mile and a half below, under the shoulder of Mount Monroe, two tiny lakes called the Lakes of the Clouds. Here they are, entirely in the open, not surrounded by any forest growth, spring fed from a subterranean source. At their elevation of five thousand feet, they may well bear the name Lakes of the Clouds, or the more poetic one sometimes given, the Hand or Mirror of Venus. These are said to make up the highest body of water in the eastern part of the country. Their overflow tumbles down the mountainside toward the base station, becoming the source of the Ammonoosuc River.

The Lakes of the Clouds serve as the water supply for the Appalachian Mountain Club's Lakes of the Clouds hut located between Mount Monroe and Mount Washington.

ON THE SUMMIT OF MOUNT WASHINGTON

"This is the second greatest show on earth" was the remark of the great showman P.T. Barnum upon viewing the wondrous outlook from Mount Washington. The mind and eye cannot appreciate on first glance the vastness of the scene. A clear day affords a view covering a radius of some 130 miles, embracing half of New England, as well as glimpses into New York and Canada. Our sense of locality is overwhelmed as we look at the outstretched landscape.

Stand a few minutes on the Summit House platform and study the details of the landscape. I am sure you saw the great Presidential peaks of Jefferson, Adams and Madison rising like huge elephants across the Great Gulf as you came up the Cog Railway or the Carriage Road. Now let your eyes travel to the east, and you'll see the Androscoggin flowing past Berlin and through the meadows of Gorham. Turn a little southerly and note the Saco Valley, North Conway and Intervale in its midst, between graceful Kearsarge and the Moat Range. A little farther away we witness the long Sandwich Range Wilderness, with the magnificent peaks of Chocorua, Paugus, Passaconaway, Whiteface, Tripyramid, Sandwich Dome and the waters of Lake Winnipesaukee in the far distance.

Seek the southern view of the little plateau that forms the summit and look down on the southern peaks of Monroe, Franklin, Clinton, Jackson and Webster. Farther away is the Franconia Range, crowned by Mount Lafayette and flanked by the noble Moosilauke. To the west lies the valley containing Fabyan's and Bretton Woods. Miles beyond is the town of Bethlehem. Against the horizon is the grand old camel's hump in Vermont. Farther north are Mansfield, Jay Peak and many other Vermont mountains, while the village of Jefferson clings to the slope of Starr King Mountain.

The Mount Washington Museum reminds the visitor that

Mount Washington rewards its admirers with early morning views bathed in pink alpine glow, with a fleeting glimpse of green flash, with a spectacular aurora or the sight of its pointed shadow touching the eastern horizon at sunset.

Now, having our bearing on the landscape from the summit, let us return to our narrative of the ascent of Mount Washington via the Cog Railway of the 1880s (begun in chapter seven) to experience what it must have been like for those early tourists who had just arrived on the summit, booked a room in the Summit House and returned to the platform of the Summit Hotel to reminisce and experience the romance of the mountain:

For some moments—moments not to be forgotten—we stood in silence. The scene was too spiritual to be grasped in a brief moment. On every side, the great mountains fell away like mists of the morning, dispersing, receding to an endless distance. Never before had such a spectacle offered itself to my eyes. The first idea was first, standing on the threshold and another planet, and second, looking down upon this world of ours outspread beneath and being face to face with eternity itself.

The bewildering throng of mountains arranged itself in chains, clusters or families. Hills drew apart, valleys opened, streams twinkled in the sun, towns and villages clung to the skirts of the mountains or dotted the rich meadows, but all was mysterious. Comprehending at last that all New England was under our feet, we began to search out certain landmarks.

What fascinated us was the sublime chaos of trenchant crests, of peaks shooting upward; and the charm of the view—such at least is the writer's conviction—resides rather in the immediate surroundings than in the extent of the panorama.

It was agreed that the one thing which struck us was the enormous mass of the mountain. The more we realized the dependent peaks, stretching eight miles north, and as many south, are nothing but buttresses, the more this prodigious weight amazes. Two long spurs, divided by the valley of the Rocky Branch, also descend into the Saco Valley as far as Bartlett, and

Climbing the White Mountains of New Hampshire

Looking south during the winter, the summit of Mount Washington is visible in the Presidential Range. The Cog tracks may be seen crossing over the summit.

another is traced between the valley of the Ammonoosuc and Israel's River. In a word, as the valleys lie and the roads run, we must travel sixty or seventy miles around in order to make the circuit of Mount Washington at its base.

The best locations for an outlook, after the Signal Station, are upon a point of rocks behind the old Tip-Top House and from the end of the hotel platform, where the railway begins its descent.

A silent movement discloses the ocean, the lakes and lowlands of Maine and New Hampshire, the broad highland of Massachusetts, the fading forms of Monadnock and Wachusett, the highest peaks of Vermont and New York and, finally, the great Canadian wilderness.

Time has dealt the mountain some crushing blows, as we see by these ghastly ruins, bearing silent testimony to their own great age. It is necessary to step with care, for the rocks may be sharp.

Noticing many boards scattered about the top and sides of the mountain, we drew our attention to them; the result of the great January gale, which had blown down the shed used as an engine house, demolished every vestige of the walk leading from the hotel to the Signal Station and distributed the fragments as if they had been straws far and wide, as we saw them.

While we were standing among the rocks, the sun touched the western horizon. The heavens became obscured. All at once we saw an immense shadow striding across the valley below us. Slowly and majestically it ascended the Carter chain until it reached the highest summit. We could not repress an exclamation of surprise; but what was our astonishment to see this immense phantom, without pausing in its progress, lift itself into the upper air to an incredible height and stand fixed and motionless high above all the surrounding mountains. It was the shadow of Mount Washington projected upon the dusky curtain of the sky. All the other peaks seem to bow their heads by a sentiment of respect, while the actual mountains exchanged majestic salutations. Then the vast gray pyramid retreated step by step into the thick shades. Night fell upon the mountain.

The expected storm, which we observed, did not fail to put in an appearance. By the time we reached the house, the wind had risen to forty miles an hour, driving the clouds in an unbroken flight against the summit, from which they rebounded with rage equal to that displayed in their vindictive onset. The Great Gulf was like the crater of some mighty volcano on the eye of an eruption, vomiting forth volumes of thickening cloud and mist. It seemed the mustering place of all the storm legions of the Atlantic, steadily pouring forth from its black jaws, unfurling their ghostly standards as they advanced to storm the battlement of the mountain. Occasionally, a break in the column disclosed the opposite peaks looming vast and black as midnight. Then the effect was indescribable. At one moment everything seemed resolving into its original elements; the next we were reminded of a gigantic cooling. The moon shed a pale light over this unearthly scene, in which creation seemed confusedly struggling.

The evening passed in comparative quiet, although the gale was moving from east to west at the rate of sixty miles an hour. Rain rattled on the roof like shots. Now and then the building shuddered and creaked, like a good ship breasting the fury of the gale. Vivid flashes of lightning made the well-lighted room momentarily dark and checked conversation as suddenly as if we had felt the electric shock. Nevertheless, the kettle sung on the stove, the telegraph instrument ticked on the table. We had Fabyan's, Littleton and White River Junction within

The Great Gulf from Mount Washington during the winter.

call. We had plenty of books, the station being well stocked from voluntary gifts. Worn out with tension of the day's activities, I crept into bed and tried to shut out the storm.

The next morning, while looking down from this eagle's nest upon the southern peaks, to where the bridle path could be distinctly traced across the plateau, and still winding on around the peaked crest of Mount Monroe, we were seized with a longing to explore the route which on a former occasion proved so difficult, but today presented apparently nothing more serious than a fatiguing scramble up and down the cone. Accordingly, taking leave of my companions, I began to feel my way down that cataract of granite, fallen, it would seem, from the sky.

Except where patches of early snow on the mountain mottled it with white, it displayed one uniform tinge of faded orange where the soft sunshine fell upon it, toned into rusty brown when overshadowed, gradually deepening to an intense bluish tone in the ravines.

Among these grasses, which speckled through the snow dusting, the Alpine flowers laid obscure, of which no species exist in the lowlands. Only the arbutus, which puts forth its pink and white flowers earlier, and is warmed into life by the snows, at all resembles them in its habits. Over this grassy plain the wind swept continually, but on putting the grass aside, the tiny blossoms had greeted us with a smile of bewitching sweetness.

These areas, extending between and sometimes surrounding the high peaks, or even approaching their summits, are the "lawns" of the botanist.

To the left, this plain, on which the grass mournfully rustled, sloped gently for approximately half a mile and then rolled heavily off, over a grass-grown rim, into Tuckerman's Ravine. In this direction the Carter Mountains appeared. Beyond, stretching away out of the plain, extended the long Boott's Spur, over which the Davis path formerly ascended from the valley of the Saco but traced with difficulty. Between this headland and Monroe opened the valley of Mount Washington River, the old Dry River of the carbuncle hunters, which the eye followed to its junction with the Saco, beyond which the precipices of Frankenstein glistened in the sun like a corselet of steel. Oakes's Gulf cuts deeply into the head of the gorge. The plain, the ravine, the spur and the gulf transmit the names of those indefatigable botanists, Bigelow, Tuckerman, Boott and Oakes.

On the other side of the ridge, the ground was more broken in its rapid descent toward the Ammonoosuc Valley, into which we looked over the right shoulder of Mount Monroe.

What a sight for the rock-wearied eye were the little Lakes of the Clouds, cuddled close to the hairy breast of the morning. On an instant the prevailing gloom was lighted as if by magic by these dainty nurslings of the clouds, which seemed innocently smiling in the face of the hideous mountain.

Retracing our way to the ridge and to the path, which we followed for some distance, we startled the silence with an occasional greeting. We descended into the hollow, where the Lakes of the Clouds seem to have checked themselves, white and still, on the very edge of the tremendous gully, cut deep into the western slopes. The lakes are the fountainhead

From the summit of Mount Washington, looking down on the landscape, clouds are seen encircling the Presidential Range.

(headwaters) of the Ammonoosuc. Their waters are too cold to nourish any species of fish; they are too elevated for any of the birds to pay them a visit.

Stone houses of refuge are much needed on the mountains over which the Crawford trail reaches the summit. They should always be provided with twigs for a fire, clean straw or boughs for a bed and printed directions for the inexperienced traveler to follow. A fireplace, furnished with a crane and a kettle for heating water, would be absolute luxuries. Being done, this fine promenade—the equal of which does not exist in New England—would be taken with confidence by numbers, instead of by the few.

It is the appropriate pendant of the ascent from the Glen by the carriage road, or from Fabyan's by the railway. One can hardly pretend to have seen the mountains in their grandest aspects until he has threaded this wondrous picture gallery, this hall of statues.

Once more we climbed the rambling and rocky stairs leading to the summit, but long before reaching it, clouds were drifting above and below us. The day was to end like so many others. The old mountain had exhausted its store of benevolence.

Time and space do not allow more than a hint of reflection of the past at all the marvels, which a few days on the mountain, with its changing atmospheric effects, would reveal. Sunrise and sunset, with their glories of color—the moonrise gilding the waters of the ocean and the intervening lakes; the sea of clouds beneath our feet with radiant sky above; the rush of the storm, wind and clouds in days of tempest; the frost feathers—each of these, when once experienced, would for years to come cling to our memories and draw us back in fancy or in reality to our much-loved White Mountains.

PATHS, ROADS AND RAIL
TO THE SUMMIT

THE WHITE HILLS

Lawrence S. Mayo, a former dean of Harvard College, was known as a scholar and student of the details of New England history. This edited essay presents one of the finest brief sketches of White Mountain history. To identify Darby Field is an easier matter than to answer the riddle of his zeal for exploration. In a private collection entitled *Three Essays*, collected by Lawrence's widow, Catherine B. Mayo, the scholar describes Field's exploration:

One Darby Field, an Irishman, living about Pascataquck, being accompanied by two Indians, went to the top of the White Hill. He made his journey in 18 days. His relation at his return was, that it was about one hundred miles from Saco, that after 40 miles travel he did, for the most part, ascend, and within 12 miles of the top was neither tree nor grass, but low vegetation, which went upon the top, but a continual ascent upon rocks, on a ridge between two valleys, filled with snow, out of which came two branches of the Saco river, which met at the foot of the hill where was an Indian town of some 200 people. Some of them accompanied him within 8 miles of the top, but durst go no further, telling him that no Indian ever dared to go higher, and that he would die if he went. So they stayed there till his return, and his two Indians took courage by his example and went with him. They traveled quickly through the thick clouds. By the way, among the rocks, there were two ponds, one a blackish water and the other reddish. The top was plain about 60 feet square. On the north side there was such a precipice, as they could scarce discern to the bottom. They had neither cloud nor wind on the top, and moderate heat. All the country about him seemed a level, except here and there a hill rising above the rest, but far beneath him. He found there much muscovy glass, they measured 40 feet long and 7 or 8 broad.

As anyone knows, this is the first record of an ascent of Mount Washington (also rendered in chapter one). Upon reflection, it is not astonishing that any white man in New England in 1642, when the struggle for mere existence was itself an adventure, should have chosen to penetrate the wilds of inland New Hampshire and climb to the summit of the forbidden heights that were piled there.

The next explorer to challenge the Presidential Range was John Josselyn, a traveler and naturalist, who wrote two small but fascinating books about seventeenth-century New England. The first, entitled *New England's Rarities Discovered*, was published in London in 1672; the second, *An Account of Two Voyages to New England*, came out in 1674. In both, Josselyn mentions the White Mountains, and it was he who first gave them the name in print. In a second visit, he was moved to explore the inland mountains that lay four score northwestward of his temporary home. Some critics have doubted that he actually visited those distant heights, upon which, he tells us, "lieth Snow all the year." But he implies that he did, and his description of the Presidential Range, which he believed to be inaccessible "but by the Gullies which the dissolved Snow hath made," varies just enough from Winthrop's account and is sufficiently detailed to carry conviction to most readers. Winthrop had spoken of the peak itself as a rock or spire. Josselyn informs us that this was called the "Sugar-loaf" and after described it as a rude heap of massie stones piled one upon another. It seems that no one but an eyewitness could have described as he does the northward view from the summit. He embellished his account by adding:

You may as you descend step as if you were going up a pair of stairs, but winding still about the Hill till you come to the top, which will require half a days time, and yet it is not above a mile, where there is also a level of about an Acre of ground, with a pond of clear water in the midst of it; which you may hear run down, but how it ascends is a mystery. The Country beyond these Hills, Northward is daunting terrible, being full of rocky Hills, as thick as Mile-hills in a Meadow, and clothed with infinite thick Woods.

With Josselyn's journey and description, the era of exploration of the White Mountains may be said to end. During this period, our ancestors had other affairs on their minds than the lure of the White Hills. Many were the expeditions of the North Country, but these were for purposes of warfare and not exploration.

It is noted, however, that other parties invaded the mountain region by following the course of the Connecticut or the Androscoggin Rivers. Only one of these ranging companies appeared to have gone up the mountains themselves. The particular excursion occurred toward the end of April 1725, when some Indian fighters climbed Mount Washington from the northwest side. As far as we know, this was the first ascent made from that area, which has since become the towns of Jefferson and Randolph. They found "snow four feet deep, but the summit was almost bare of snow, though covered with white frost and ice; a small pond of water, near the top, was hard frozen."

To this list of adventurers we add Nicholas Austin. In June 1774, a crew of men, who were making a road through the Pinkham Notch, felt the urge to make the ascent—and make it they did. Apparently they went by way of Tuckerman's Ravine, for they brought back reports of "a body of snow thirty feet deep, and so hard, as to bear them." About two weeks later, some of the same group, including Captain Evans of Conway, repeated the trip and found the snow only five feet deep. As far as we know, for almost fifty years no one had felt the call to go to the top, and then in the year 1774, one after the other penetrated the woods, struggled up the ravines and made his way over the loose rocks to the summit of Mount Washington.

Jeremy Belknap, a minister at Dover and the future founder of the Massachusetts Historical Society, was not only a naturalist but also a historian and wrote a *History of New Hampshire*, which remains a classic among works of its kind. It was Belknap who opened the period of the pursuit of natural history in the White Mountains. Like most educated men of his day, he had a strong interest in the fauna, flora and minerals with which the Creator had surrounded mankind. Governor Wentworth, for example, wrote to a young friend whose duty required him to explore the New England wilderness:

> *If any curiosities, natural or artificial, should come in your way, remember that I am still disposed to exchange good gold for almost anything that may employ my mind to discover, or my time to improve the use or improvement of, from the humblest pebble to the most wonderful animal.*

In Jeremy Belknap's case, there was not only this childlike curiosity but also a special reason for studying the highlands of New Hampshire. In those

Above: The Pinkham Notch Camp of the Appalachian Mountain Club, located at an elevation of 2,040 feet, is high enough to ensure permanent snow from November through April. This is the nearest camp in the state to the Tuckerman Ravine Ski Area, where the snows last well into June.

Left: A fine example of the snowdrifts in Crawford Notch in the White Mountains.

days, a historian must make his readers acquainted with the natural history of his subject, as well as with its political, economic and social development. Belknap intended to devote an entire volume to it in his forthcoming work. He must examine the White Mountains himself.

Consequently, early in the summer of 1784, he organized a party of six or seven congenial gentlemen, plus two college students, and on horseback they set out for the Eastern Notch and the top of the highest mountain. The expedition became an epoch in the history of the region, and the story of it is almost too well known to bear retelling it here. Still, there is always freshness to it, and I cannot let it pass with a mere mention.

Belknap and his friends went up to Pinkham Notch to the watershed, a few miles south of the Glen House, and set up their base camp of operation near a beaver meadow. After spending a cool evening there, Belknap and his friend Cutler intended to ascertain the exact height of Mount Washington. But the barometers in 1784 were not pocket affairs that could be carried about with convenience. Theirs was an old-fashioned mercury barometer consisting of a glass tube about three feet long that protruded from a leather bag filled with mercury. Consequently, when Cutler made his calculations, he found the altitude of the mountain to be nine thousand feet instead of an early estimate of sixty-two hundred. But even this computation did not satisfy Belknap. After his struggle on the mountainside, he may well have thought that twenty thousand would have been nearer the correct incident. In his *History of New Hampshire*, Belknap referred to the accident that made accurate measurement impossible and stated his conviction that whenever the mountain could be measured "with the required precision," it would be found to "exceed ten thousand feet, of perpendicular altitude, above the level of the ocean."

One is not surprised to learn that Jeremy Belknap, who was short and fat, and another member of the party, who was far from rugged, gave out long before the tree line was reached. Even though Belknap could not make it to the top, we are inclined to attribute to him the naming of the peak Mount Washington. In the third volume of his *History of New Hampshire*, which was published in 1792, he mentions the ascent of 1784 and says that the mountain "has lately been distinguished by the name of Mount Washington." As this is the first time that the name appears in print, and as we know that Belknap was a great admirer of our first president, we are probably justified in assuming that it was he who christened it so. In 1796, the name appeared on a German map of New Hampshire, and in 1797 Timothy Dwight, the much-traveled president of Yale College, mentioned Mount Washington in a letter as if the name had become well established.

Manasseh Cutler, who accompanied Belknap to the mountains in 1784, was one of those versatile Yankees who helped to make New England what it is. So it came to pass that in 1804, just twenty years later, he was again on the road to Conway and points north. As Belknap had died in the meantime, Cutler chose for his associates Professor William D. Peck of Harvard (a botanist), Nathaniel Bowditch (author of the *Navigator*) and several others. They made the ascent on July 28 of that year. Peck and the botanists, to their hearts' content, returned to Cambridge with a number of interesting specimens for the herbarium, though Peck had the misfortune to lose half his collection.

In the wake of Cutler and Peck, many botanists found their way to Mount Washington during the next half century, and their names have become permanently associated with various part of the mountain. Bigelow's Lawn—the nearly level expanse between the crags and the cone, which the early explorers called the plain—commemorates Dr. Jacob Bigelow, who scaled the heights in 1816. With him was a gentleman by the name Dr. Francis Boott, a botanical friend whose name still clings to a formidable elevation known as Boott's Spur. Later came William Oakes, for whom Oakes's Gulf, a large chasm south of Bigelow's Lawn, was named. We should not forget Professor Edward Tuckerman of Amherst College, who made his first visit to the mountains in 1837 and whose name is not likely to be forgotten by anyone who has climbed the steep walls of Tuckerman's Ravine. In earlier days, this part of the mountain was known as Hardscrabble.

This scene of the Presidential Range and Mount Washington was drawn by I. Sprague for Oakes's *White Mountain Scenery*, 1848.

A 1910 view of Mount Starr as seen from Whitefield, New Hampshire.

The Carriage (Auto) Road on Mount Washington leads to the summit. During the late nineteenth century, the road was popular for the horse-drawn buggy. In the distance are Mount Adams and Mount Madison.

William Oakes died in 1848, and perhaps that date is a good one to mark the end of the era of pursuit of natural history in the White Mountains.

Between 1800 and 1840, artists and painters became hungry for natural scenery that would please and inspire them with reverence for the natural beauty of the state.

It appears that of all the visitors to the White Mountains in these past centuries, Starr King was undoubtedly the most blessed, for he felt the thrill of the romanticist, the quiet ecstasy of the aesthete and the deep rapture of the religious man. One thing is certain: the atmosphere of romance has retreated farther into the White Hills. It refuses to be found near the main highway of our present day. It disturbs the visitor who loves the mountains to discover that the more recent writers fail to share or sense the emotion that lies behind every chapter of King's *White Hills*. Their only reaction is to accuse King of what they may call spiritual intoxication. I have come to believe that the White Mountains of the nineteenth century are invisible to the eyes of the twenty-first century. It may be that thousands now enjoy, in one way or another, what only hundreds enjoyed in a very different way a few decades ago.

With Horse and Wagon

This is a story of the first team driven to the summit of Mount Washington as narrated by John Olsen. John Olsen, a former councilor of topography and exploration, is not only familiar with the White Mountains, but also has long been a collector of White Mountain literature and is acquainted with many relatively unknown facets of this interesting field. The following account appeared in a letter printed in the *Boston Journal* of July 16, 1861:

> *To the Editor of* The Boston Journal:
> *I sent you a line this morning at mail closing, to say that an attempt was at that moment being made to reach the summit of Mount Washington with a horse and wagon. I write now to say that this remarkable feat has been accomplished successfully by Mr. J.M. Thompson, the proprietor of the Glen House, and he has returned with horse and wagon all safe and sound. Getting wind that a Boston gentleman was preparing early next week to drive to the "Tip-Top House," Mr. Thompson with only one man on horseback* [his blacksmith] *to accompany him, started from the Glen House at 4 o'clock this morning with his famous mountain horse*

Climbing the White Mountains of New Hampshire

"Sorrel Tom" harnessed in an ordinary Concord wagon without once un-harnessing or in any way, and returned in the same manner.

Nine hours was consumed in the adventure, from the start at the Glen to the return, including some two hours spent mostly in the thick fog on the summit. People who want to enjoy the ride, as none by Thompson did, must come to the Glen and hear him "tell it."

Seven or eight chairs and a couple of Piazza columns are but part of the illustrations, which it takes to help along in the incident. The landlord's graphic description of how he went and how he brought up in the ride, the horse and wagon, too, came bodily into the narrative; the former has scarcely a scratch upon him, whereas the wagon wheels look as if they had been kept tally on with a Mount Washington boulder in the hands of a Titan. Of course the carriage road gave Mr. Thompson easy passage to within a mile of the summit; to overcome the last mile was the tug. He passed over a space of nearly two miles of horizontals and perpendiculars to span this one-mile in going up, and more than this in coming down, for it was impossible for him to descend with his team over many places in his track or ascent. "Sorrel Tom" would generally drag the wagon after him when he got his footholds to suit him; but in descending it took the three, counting in Tom himself to keep the wagon from tumbling over the horse.

Of the two, horse and driver, the horse that hauled a wagon after him up the cone of Mount Washington is entitled to the most credit. Mt. Thompson himself decided and yet "Sorrell Tom" did not "lag a hair," neither did he show any fatigue. In fact, all along over this terrific climbing the utmost good faith between the two was necessary, for often when Thompson would be "prospecting" about for where next to start, the instinct of the animal would be aroused, and he would step from rock to rock wholly unguided, and safely get over the most difficult places.

The carriage road will be done—passage for wagons—to the Lizzie Bourne monument, within 20 rods of the top of the mountain, by the first week in August, if the weather is good.

W

"Into Cloudland by Cars"

The following article, "Into Cloudland by Cars," was published in *Harper's Weekly* on August 21, 1869, by an unknown writer. However, it is worthy of presenting at this time for it reflects the romance and adventure of the

Cog Railway traveling the western side of Mount Washington during the late 1800s:

We started (six of us, including our driver), after an early breakfast at Littleton, hoping to reach the foot of Mount Washington in time for an afternoon train to the summit.

Our twenty mile ride, with the grand mountains rising before us, changing in form with every turn of the winding road, swelling and subsiding like gigantic sea waves, as the varying cloud-shadows moved across them, had intensified all our previous desires, and the ladies vowed with great vehemence that to the top they would go, though they should do it upon their hands and knees. And so it seemed they must, for when we reached the toll-gate at the commencement of the turnpike, near the old Fabyan stand, the good natured gate-keeper, with many sympathetic regrets, said the car had gone up. A glance at our disappointed faces indeed a doubtful "perhaps they may go up again this afternoon." This, with a tin cup of delicious mountain strawberries, which he had just gathered, gave us some encouragement. On we went, by the beautiful Ammonoosuc, calculated our chances, and watching the thread on the mountain, scarcely believing it possible anything more than Queen Mab's fairy coach could descend upon it, but each moment hoping to see the smoke, which would show us the train was descending, and might therefore be ready to take us up.

Arriving at the depot, a busy scene met our eyes; piles of lumber, newly erected sheds, workmen going and coming and plying the hammer and the saw, but, alas! No cars. We went into the log cabin, where the ladies were amused to find telegraph office, storm room, parlor, and sleep room in a curious state of admixture, where we were informed that the superintendent of the road, Mr. J.J. Sanborn, would soon be down with the train from the summit. We found here Mr. Marsh, the projector of the road, and from him gained some idea of what an undertaking it had been. When, twenty years ago, he applied for a charter from the New Hampshire Legislature, a worthy member proposed to amend Mr. Marsh's petition by substituting "the moon" for the top of Mount Washington. Where is that member, and those who laughed with him?

Mr. Marsh obtained his charter, purchased 17,000 acres of land from the base to the summit, broke ground, and built a mile of the road before railroad men could be convinced of its practicability.

Then a company was formed, and under Mr. J.J. Sanborn, the present Superintendent, the work slowly but surely progressed. Driven away from their work early in the fall, and not able to recommence until another summer was almost at hand, there were very few weeks of each year in which any work could be done. Last October the laborers were interrupted by a sudden snowstorm without having time to gather up their tools. Under the snow they laid all winter, and not until June could the men go up to lay the remaining five hundred feet of track. In less than a month it was completed; and by the opening of another season there will be a comfortable depot and a small hotel at the foot.

We took our lunch, sheltered from the sun, and partially protected from the numerous black flies, in one of the rough buildings put up for the workmen. We availed ourselves of the opportunity to study a little the construction of the cars and track, and carried off some of Kilburn Brothers, admirable stereoscopic pictures, which, transferred by the artist to these pages, give the result of our investigations better than we can do in words.

This is a fine stereoscopic view of the Mount Washington Cog locomotive No. 9 Waumbek as seen near the top of the mountain.

THE MOUNT WASHINGTON COG RAILWAY

A third track, laid between the other two, is fitted with cogs. A third wheel, both in the engine and the cars, is furnished in like manner. The teeth of the one fitting into those of the other propel both cars and engine steadily up the steepest grade. It thus differs from the Mount Holyoke Railway, where a stationary engine pulls you up by a long rope, and from the Mount Cenis Railway, where two little wheels, griping the third rail, propel you by means of friction only. Looking up the track, and realizing that it is really as steep in some places as an ordinary flight of stairs, we almost doubted our courage, and we listened eagerly to Mr. Marsh's kind and detailed explanations of the means which are used to secure the safety of the train. More than once the ladies shook their heads and turned away from the track, made almost dizzy with looking at it from below. Hark! A whistle! We run to see a black dot smoking a very minute cigar. It comes nearer, and, as we see men and women there, we hold our breath, and when they safely reach us, strangers though they are, we feel like congratulating them that they have safely passed through such an awful experience. We are somewhat rebuffed by seeing them step calmly out upon the platform as if from an ordinary carriage. We are not willing to be outdone, so we think of the atmospheric brakes, of the friction-brakes, of the ratchet-wheel, and the cogs, and look very brave. Mr. Sanborn, in spite of some difficulties in the way, most kindly made up a special train. The old and smaller engine, and a common platform car, with a rough tier of seat upon it, were soon ready. The seats were arranged to be level on an ascent of one foot in five, and when the car is on level ground the seats present that angle. While we were arranging ourselves upon them our predecessors on the road stood by giving us the benefit of their recent experience—counseling sundry trying on the hats, coat-buttoning, and extra wrappings. But the sun is so hot! Never mind; wait and see how long it will be so.

We start. There are no words—only looks, at one another, and underhand grasping of the seat; and up, up we go, as if pushed from the earth into the air. No place to step off upon. On a trestlework, sometimes more than twenty feet high, we seem entirely severed from the earth. The stoutest of the party looks a little pale; but we feel the firm grip of cog upon cog; we remember that the wheel is so clamped upon the pin-rigged middle rail that neither the engine nor the car can be lifted or thrown off; that the pawl dropped into the ratchet-wheel would hold us in the steepest place; that the shutting of the valve in the atmospheric brakes effectually stops the wheels from moving, we look at our Superintendent, who stands composedly watching the engine, his calmness inspires us with courage, and we dare to

Climbing the White Mountains of New Hampshire

No trip is complete without this long-remembered climb to the summit of Mount Washington by the Cog Railway. Seen here is a trainload of passengers enjoying some of nature's best workmanship.

look off, and then—we forget all fears. We are ascending so precipitately that unless we look directly behind us up the track, we seem to go up from the middle of a great valley. Hills and valleys, streams and lakes and distant villages, spread out before us and beguiles us of all fear.

Suddenly we become conscious that there are no more black flies. The sun seems not so hot. Our wrappings are not quite so oppressive. The trees are not so large. We are still creeping up. There are no level places. When we stop to water the engine, it is on a steep grade, and we wonder whether we shall not go whizzing down. But no! We start again, and still up we go. The horizon extends. The trees appear smaller, the flowers are such as bloomed with us two months ago. Admiration gives place to awe. There is no room in our hearts for fear. We care not if the wind is chilly—we drink in the wonder. Another stop for water is short. Why? Frozen up. Frozen up in July? Sure enough soon we come to a laborer with red, cold hands, who reports frozen ground only a foot below to surface. Think of it, you who were sweltering in the city. But look off: Yonder are distant lakes, lifted up by the sunlight. The mountains about us shrink into small hills, and still we are not at the top. It begins to feel damp. We come to a cloud. What is it like? Like rain? No. Like fog? No. We are saturated, permeated with moisture. It seems almost to drive through us. But now it lifts, and how gloriously the sun lights up the valleys! There are no trees

This is an excellent view of the summit of Mount Washington with the Tip-Top House on the left and the Summit House on the right.

about us, only dwarfed attempts at trees. Now only moss-covered rocks, now bare rocks. Just beside us winds the carriage road. Now we pass poor Lizzie Bourne's rude but most appropriate monument. Now we are at the top. Cloud-wrapped, we see nothing save the rocks just about us. Stepping off the car we are almost thrown down by the wind. Tightly drawing our wraps about us, shutting the driving water out of our eyes, we scramble to the Tip-Top House, and by the blazing fire we have time to consider what we have done.

In an hour and a half, we have climbed by steam a ladder nearly three miles long. We have ascended in that time over 3,600 feet. We are more than 6,000 feet above the level of the sea. We have passed from the atmosphere of July to that of January. The stunted vegetation just below is not that of New England. It is the vegetation of Labrador. Shall we dare to go down again, to drop, in some long grades, at the rate of one foot in three? The Superintendent tells that a car set free would make the descent in less than three minutes. We shudder at the bare thought. He tells us that he can load that car with stone, adjust the brakes, and leave it without a man to operate them, and it will make the descent in safety. We are reassured. There are the atmospheric brakes—if one gives way there and three more to hold; there is an ordinary friction brake with which the engineer tells us he can stop the train in four inches; there is the ratchet-wheel that stops it instantly; and

Climbing the White Mountains of New Hampshire

there is the steam in the engine, never used in the descent, but always ready as an additional protection; and finally, the mechanism is so adjusted that it seems as though not even carelessness in the engineer could well be fatal. It is only the novelty of the situation, which inspires fear. The novelty is already gone, and after a good breakfast we descend the mountainside, exchanging the piercing winds and yet more penetrating clouds for sunlight, throwing off our wintry wrappings, coming from the region of barren rocks to that of stunted vegetation, and from that of stunted vegetation to that of noble forest trees, with less tremor than we often have experienced on the top of an old-fashioned stage among the precipitous hills of Maine.

THE GREAT FIRE ON MOUNT WASHINGTON

On the evening of June 18, 1908, fire broke out in the Mount Washington Summit House and, fanned by a high wind, made a clean sweep of almost every building on the summit, together with the railway platform and over two hundred feet of track. Totally destroyed were the hotel, the help's cottage, the stage office, the printing office of *Among the Clouds*, the train shed and the U.S. Signal Station. The only building spared on the summit itself was the Tip-Top House, thanks to its stone wall and the fact that the wind here drove the flames away from the roof. This last circumstance was also the saving of the two stables, which lay some distance below the summit.

The hotel was unoccupied at the time, not being scheduled to open until June 29. However, it seems that a work party, under the direction of the superintendent of the railway, had been there that day, preparing the railway and hotel for the opening. This party had left for the base station at about 5:00 p.m., after disconnecting the telephone, which it had installed. The only persons left on the summit were a group of young people from Berlin, who had walked over the range from the Madison Hut and were settled for the evening in the stage office. When members of this party saw the flames breaking from a window in the hotel, they forced their way into the building in the hope of putting out the fire but found that it had already gained too much headway. Unable to make use of the telephone, they had already been seen both by the Fabyan House and the Glen House but not the base station, which lay too close under the mountain. A train started up from the base station, and a team headed out from the Glen House. Both arrived in time to see the fire at its height and were in fact obliged to remain at some distance from the summit.

The most complete description of the fire that has come down to us was contained in a special edition of *Among the Clouds* in August 1908, edited and published by Frank H. Burt and printed at the base station.

TROLLEY ON THE PRESIDENTIAL RANGE

Excerpts from the following account have been provided by Francis Belcher, executive director of the Appalachian Mountain Club (AMC) in 1957. Earlier, he was a hut man at Pinkham Notch and Madison. From 1936 to 1956, he held positions in the legal department of the Boston & Maine Railroad, where he became familiar with many of the interesting facts mentioned in this article:

The dreams of New England's Railroad tycoon of the early 20th century, Charles S. Mellen, reached their peak in a plan which was legally embraced under the innocent title of Extension of the Mount Washington Branch of the Concord and Montreal Railroad. When this plan was unfolded in the period between 1910 and 1913 and its supporters were looking for an aspiring name for the extension, it came close to being called The Mount Washington and Great Range Railway.

The search for a proper name on the part of the Boston & Maine Railroad's high authorities prompted Allen Chamberlain, noted AMC member and former club president, to write, on April 16, 1912, to Edgar J. Rich, general solicitor of the Boston & Maine and himself a club member, as follows:

The madam [Mrs. Chamberlain] is jubilant over the prospect of the project's completion within her lifetime, of the scenic railway on the Great Range.

I can't say that I share her enthusiasm for this project. I confess that it was my hope that the work would prove to be too expensive to warrant construction. Your inquiry as to the suitability of a certain name for the road is discouraging, for it looks as if the thing is progressive.

"Mount Washington and Great Range Railway" seems suitable to me, though I would substitute for the word "Railway" the phrase "Scenery Smasher."

What, then, was this Scenery Smasher? What was its background and its details? From whom did it come, and now, some forty years later, where did it go?

Climbing the White Mountains of New Hampshire

By 1900, the Boston & Maine Railroad, by various methods, had taken control of most of the rail lines in the state of New Hampshire. Under this control, through a lease of the Concord & Montreal Railroad in 1895, came the famous Mount Washington Cog Railway, the summit circle fifty rods in diameter and the Summit and Tip-Top Houses. The Summit House burned flat in 1908, leaving only the inadequate Tip-Top House to care for the many tourists who visited New Hampshire's most famous summer attraction.

While Charles S. Mellen had received his early railroad training in the Granite State, later his interest turned south to the more lucrative territory served by the New York, New Haven & Hartford Railroad. There, with the help of J.P. Morgan, he tied together a gigantic monopoly of transportation, including virtually every boat, rail and trolley line in southern New England. By the year 1907, this was not enough for Mellen and Morgan. Their eyes turned north again, and in the spring of that year they acquired a controlling interest in the stock of the Boston & Maine by exchanging New Haven shares for those of the Boston & Maine.

It didn't take long for the fertile minds of Mellen and New Hampshire's railroad titan Benjamin A. Kimball to evolve a dream for the future greatness of New England's highest peak, Mount Washington. This dream reached the point of action in 1911, as the article provided by Belcher continued:

On July 4, of that year, they were ready. Surveyors were sent out that day from the Base Station to find a route for their dream, a twenty-mile electric railroad or trolley line that would end at a proposed breath-taking stone-and-steel hotel on the top of the mountain. For two years the efforts of these and many other New Haven and Boston & Maine officials and employees were directed toward the realization of this dream. Architects and draftsmen worked in New Haven and Boston, lawyers and financiers planned and argued in Concord, Boston, New Haven and Washington. Skilled workmen were busy at Marshfield, while surveyors toiled on the project.

The dream called for a single-track location that would travel from Fabyan to the Base Station and thence to Caps Ridge at Jefferson Notch. From there the line would proceed by loops and switchbacks over the Castellated Ridge to gain enough altitude to pass to the south around Mount Jefferson and hear for Mount Washington, which had to be looped on the upper part of the cone to allow the line to come to its end at a spacious platform in front of the great and glorious hotel.

What were some of the causes that had set this airy dream into being? We must look at a prosperous era and examine it:

> *Railroads had more than come of age by 1910. Electric Trolley lines had started later than their steam brothers, but were fast catching up. By 1911, they were being run almost everywhere that steam lines were not. They were considered cheaper, cleaner, and they didn't start fires, a matter of particular importance in the wooded mountains. The consolidation of New England's major railroads under the control of the dynamic, spectacular and controversial Mellen meant their management by a strong advocate of electric traction lines. Behind this advocate stood the might house of Morgan.*

Summertime accommodations on the summit of Mount Washington were cramped, to say the least, after the disastrous Summit House fire of 1908. With each passing summer, it became more obvious that the owners would have to provide some replacement. Meanwhile, the Cog Railway had been suffering for some time from improper maintenance. To return it to adequate condition would require considerable capital. This was no time to pour new money after old.

The final incentive came with the passage of the Weeks Act in 1911. The proposed creation of a national forest in the White Mountains, as soon as practicable, brought with it new dangers to the dream. A tour de force was needed. The Boston & Maine Railroad must get title to the desired right of way while the needed lands were still owned by the Berlin Timberland Company and the Conway Company, both large customers of the Boston & Maine Railroad:

> *On July 4, 1911, preceded and followed for day by a publicity fanfare of symphonic proportions, an engineering crew started from Marshfield to look for a practical and scenic route to Mount Washington, to replace the worn three-and-one-half mile direct ascent then and now taken by the familiar "puffin' devils." Meanwhile architects had drawn plans for a new and spacious hotel, and lawyers were working out financial plans and petitioning for proper approvals.*

The first group of civic engineers numbered seventeen. The route for which they searched could have no more than a 6 percent grade at any point. With this in mind, they began their efforts at the top:

Climbing the White Mountains of New Hampshire

Daily they rode to the summit by the first morning train and worked downhill. The grade on the summit cone was to be controlled by two complete circuits of the mountain, which necessitated two crossings at grade of the Carriage Road. By this time their route had reached a point close to the present junction of the Southside Trail and the Crawford Path on the southwesterly side of the mountain. Later, the crew was supplemented by other surveyors who worked with them. Eventually, all transits were sighted on Mount Jefferson, and there the two groups joined after a summer and a half of heavy work. A route was finally punched through.

The surveyors' plans called for the electric line to start at the Fabyan House, from which point the Boston & Maine Railroad was then operating a steam train shuttle service to the base station. The trolley route followed this existing line to the base, where it turned abruptly left and ran north to Jefferson Notch. The description of the line from this point on can best be given by quoting a story that appeared daily in *Among the Clouds* throughout the summer of 1912:

From Jefferson Notch...the road crosses what is known as the Ridge of Caps...Five hundred feet higher the road comes to the very edge of the Castellated Ridge, and here will be one of the most interesting features of the journey. Instead of making a turn around the edge of the ridge, the railway will go through the ridge by a tunnel, and with a turn to the left will come out and cross itself.

On the west slope of Mount Jefferson, beginning at the Castellated Ridge, the route presented great difficulties, making it necessary to put in two switchbacks...After the road passes over itself it runs back toward the Base Station, but always climbing, for a mile and a half. At the first switchback there is a sheer drop in front of nearly a thousand feet. The car will then run backward to the Castellated Ridge and the second switchback.

The foregoing was the official language of the railroad's press release and was quoted in many metropolitan papers of the day. It was an understatement to say that one tunnel through the Castellated Ridge and two switchbacks between this and Caps Ridge were interesting features. Anyone familiar with this terrain and its steepness would be startled at this section of the safe and scenic route:

From the second switchback the cars would then run in a southerly direction along the west side of Mount Jefferson, passing nine hundred feet below its summit, then travel the western slope of Mount Clay, parallel to and not far from the present course of the Gulf-side Trail. The location continued to follow this southerly course and crossed the existing Cog Railway track near the Gulf Tanks. Then it ran to the south across the lower west slope of the cone of Mount Washington to the point previously mentioned (what is now the junction of the Southside Trail and the Crawford Path.)

Meanwhile, the Boston & Maine's legal staff was hard at work interviewing the property owners of the lands that would be needed and, more important, negotiating their price. Most of the land was owned by the Conway Company, the Brown Company's realty subsidiary, and the Berlin Timberland Company. Again a quote from *Among the Clouds* (August 15, 1912) provides insight:

E.O. Woodward, Boston & Maine Conveyors, Assistant, Engineer H.S. Jewell Survey Chief of the Boston & Maine Railroad, H.G. Spaulding of the Mount Washington Railway, and L.D. Goulding and G.D. Thompson of the Conway Company went to make an examination of land takings for the railway location and hotel site. The area at the summit is fifty rods in radius and the new location will require twice as much. In the afternoon the party took a tramp from Base Station to Jefferson Notch and Castellated Ridge to determine the land required of the Conway Company.

According to the surveyors' plans:

A total of 171.02 acres would have to be purchased to provide for a location or right of way 99 feet wide, the loop, two switchbacks on the Great Range, and the hotel site on Mount Washington. Of this total 130.18 acres in eight separate parcels were owned by the Conway Company, and 39.16 acres in five parcels by the Berlin Timberland Company, and 1.68 acres in two parcels by other persons. The president of the Conway Company was a friend and business associate of Mellen.

Since the secretary of agriculture by right of the Week's Act of 1911 was also interested in procuring this entire vast area as a start for a new national forest, the owners were in an interesting position. Results of this will be seen later.

Climbing the White Mountains of New Hampshire

An artist's view of the proposed Summit Hotel and the trolley circling the summit of the mountain.

On July 22, 1912, the New Hampshire Public Service Commission made possible one more step toward the realization of this project by making available a plan to finance it. They granted permission to the lessor-owner, the Concord and Montreal Railroad, to construct this "Extension." The matter of the insurance of $1,500,000 in stock was not ruled on at this hearing, and according to railroad records was to be arranged by the railroad as work progressed. Mellen never worried about methods of finance until necessary.

During all this time, what was being planned for the top of Mount Washington? The architect's sketch shows that it was an imposing structure. The railroad's publicists used elegant language, calling it

Unique among hotels, The only hotel in the world...to have a mountain top through its floor, Every room an outside room, One hundred sleeping rooms, Entire hotel a circular observatory one hundred and fifty feet in diameter, Glass skylight ninety feet in diameter above a searchlight...of sufficient power to be seen from Portland, Inside verandas...Having the very summit protrude through the first floor so that one may stand on the summit and view all but 48 degrees of the 360-degree view.

The plans were the work of New Haven's noted architect R.C. Reamer, who had gained fame for designing hotels in Yellowstone Park. The building was to be a massive structure of stone, steel, concrete and glass, since experience then indicated "that wood would not be able to withstand the elements, and plenty of solid material being already at hand." How different this would be from the club's experience in constructing exposed huts at that time and in later years!

The station platform was on the south side of the hotel and summit. Two entrances led from it to the basement of the hotel, one for passengers, and the other for freight and provisions. Passengers went through their entrance and reached the lobby by a flight of stairs or by an elevator up one floor. The main dining room was on the first floor, above the platform entrance section, in the 48-degree area of blocked view as one stood on the center summit rocks. In this sumptuous room it was planned to care for daily eating needs of 300 to 400 guests. Kitchens, wine room, barber shop, billiard room, boiler and other service rooms were in the basement area.

Down below, at the base station, activity was increasing in other directions:

A large modern hotel on the top demanded among other thing a vital commodity that the upper part of the mountain couldn't supply in sufficient quantity: water. In anticipation of the planned building, steps were taken in 1911 to create an enlarged pumping station that would—and did—force the Ammonoosuc's clear water under very heavy pressure, all the way to the summit in one lift, a height difference of about 3,700 feet.

Work on this station was begun on September 7, 1911, by a Boston & Maine bridge and building crew. The structure was located some twenty-five feet from the track in the vicinity of the laundry building. It housed two Dean Brothers steam pumps with steam cylinders sixteen inches in diameter and a large steam boiler. The new three and one half mile water line to the top was made of double thick piping 1½ inches in interior diameter. Despite what happens to other phases of this "Extension," this one was completed in 1912 and went to work shortly thereafter. At least there would be and has been water on top for the railroad and the present buildings.

The power that would generate the electricity for the traction line was planned for on paper. A large steam generating plant was designed for erection at the Base Station. A transmission feeder line to give extra juice for the cars was also planned for installation between Jefferson Notch and the south end of the upper line on the west side of the cone of Mount Jefferson.

Climbing the White Mountains of New Hampshire

By the end of the summer of 1912, progress was obvious. The final issue of *Among the Clouds* for that year (September 14, 1912) summed it up this way:

We take pleasure in informing our reader that a vast amount of work has been accomplished. The working out of preliminary details, such as surveying the right of way, making changes in the line that would be beneficial for grades and curves, and measurements for bridges and trestles have occupied the engineering corps all summer on the ground, as well as the legal and other departments of the railroad in taking over the right of way from different landowners who control this section of the country. By another season everything undoubtedly will be in readiness so that construction can begin...The railroad officials have entered into the matter with enthusiasm, and Supt. Cummings in particular has devoted himself to the undertaking heart and soul.

The year 1912 witnessed the high-water mark in actual work done for the dream and hopes of the backers on this extension. While time remained, survey crews worked into the fall to check all the angles and level the grades for the big push that would start in the spring. It was during this work on September 18, 1912, that a portent of the end of the project might have been observed in the mysterious disappearance and death of John M. Keenan, a rod man from Charlestown, Massachusetts. Keenan had been at work on the upper part of the cone of the mountain. It was his first day, and apparently alarmed when the peak suddenly became cloud-capped, he disappeared downhill. A thorough search failed to locate him. Two days later, half crazed, he was seen by three separate groups along the road in Pinkham Notch near the Glen House. One party actually gave him a ride south for two miles and let him out at his request near an old logging camp. Despite a further search by hundreds of volunteers, no trace of him was ever found.

With this unfortunate event, all crews were pulled of the hill. Work in the field on the extension was finished for 1912, and for all times.

The final chapter in the history of the scenic railway may be told in various ways. But they all center on the crumbling of Mellen's vast New England transportation empire. In 1913, one of his last additions to the empire, the Boston & Maine, became the first to feel the weight of financial doom, and with the Boston & Maine's collapse went the extension of the Mount Washington Branch of the Concord & Montreal Railroad.

The first issue of *Among the Clouds* for 1913 (July 11, 1913) announced the following:

We regret to state that the work on the summit has been indefinitely postponed, which is probably due to financial conditions. However, as soon as this and other matters are straightened out, the new railway and hotel will in all probability be built.

This is an interesting and conservative explanation and raises the question of what the other matters were that needed straightening out.

Previously mentioned were the passage of the Weeks Act and the attendant possibility of the purchase of the Presidential Range lands to form a part of a new national forest. During the fall and winter season of 1912–13, U.S. Department of Agriculture representatives on the one hand and those of the Berlin and Conway Companies on the other consummated agreements to sell all the lands through which the Boston & Maine planned to run its new line. There is reason to suspect that the owners anticipated the Boston & Maine's eventual financial crisis in making their decision to sell to the government. This event left the railroad only two doubtful avenues by which to get its right of way to the top: 1) an act of Congress or 2) modified tripartite agreements between the parties to permit the extension through government lands. While both avenues were considered by New Haven and Boston & Maine officials, the possibility of success by either was so questionable that further action was dropped with the financial crisis in 1913.

The long and formal report of the investigation by the Interstate Commerce Commission in 1914 into the affairs of the New Haven Railroad, its many subsidiaries and appendages and Messrs. Mellen and Morgan, etc., gives a final explanation for the demise of the extension:

The New Haven System has more than three hundred subsidiary corporations in a web of entangling alliances...The result of our research has been to disclose one of the most glaring instances of mal-administration revealed in all the history of American railroading. Marked features and significant incidents in the loose, extravagant, and improvident administration of the finances of the New Haven as shown in this investigation are the Boston and Maine Railroad despoilment...The domination of all the affairs of this railroad by Mr. Morgan and Mr. Mellen.

According to this long and thorough report, the Boston & Maine Railroad and its many subsidiaries, including the Mount Washington Cog Railway, emerged from this mill of manipulation by Mellen & Co. physical and financial losers.

Climbing the White Mountains of New Hampshire

An aerial view of the Summit House Hotel during the mid-twentieth century, with the TV Station, the Auto Road and the U.S. Weather Observatory, on the summit of Mount Washington, New England's highest peak.

A committee of two, appointed by the Appalachian Mountain Club Council in 1912 to look into the matter, had the words directly from Mr. Mellen himself as a result of a conference in March 1913. The councilor of improvements, Dr. Harry W. Tyler, and the vice-president, Walter Jenney, officially reported their interview in club council records as follows:

> *Dr Tyler for the Committee for the Preservation of the Tip-Top House reported an interview with President Mellen of the New York, New Haven and Hartford Railroad by himself and Mr. Jenney at which Mr. Mellen had stated that on account of the desperate condition of the finances of the Boston and Maine Railroad nothing would be done on Mount Washington either with respect to the proposed scenic railway or the hotel.*

Thus ended the work of many hands and the spending of large sums toward the dream of a few. This was the end: no looping electric necklace, no concrete crown. The high ridges and alpine areas of the Great Range fortunately never met this Scenery Smasher.

Appendix A

CHRONOLOGY OF HISTORIC EVENTS

Mount Washington

1642	Darby Fields and two Indian guides were credited with the first ascent of Mount Washington.
1784	The Belknap and Cutler expedition conducted the first scientific research on the Presidential Range.
1792	The name Mount Washington appeared in print for the first time in Jeremy Belknap's *History of New Hampshire*.
1819	Dr. Jacob Bigelow and Dr. Francis Boott (and company) toured the mountain. Barometric measurements were made by these gentlemen to ascertain the summit's elevation: 6,250 feet.
1819	Abel and Ethan Allen Crawford constructed a footpath over the Presidential Range.
1821	The Crawfords constructed a second path up the mountain. Today, this route follows the present trail of the Cog Railway.
1840	Abel Crawford was the first to ride a horse to the summit via the Crawford Path (First Bridal Path) at age seventy-five.
1844	Nathaniel Davis opened the new fifteen-mile Bridle Path from the lower Crawford Notch along the Montalban Ridge to the summit of Mount Washington.
1850	The First Glen House was built on the eastern side of Mount Washington near Pinkham Notch.
1852	The First Summit House hotel was constructed on the summit of Mount Washington.

1853	The second summit hotel, the Tip-Top House, opened to the public.
1853	The Mount Washington Carriage (Auto) Road was chartered.
1854	An observatory was erected on the summit of Mount Washington.
1855	Lizzie Bourne was the first woman to perish on the mountain.
1861	The Mount Washington Summit Road Company completed construction of the Carriage (Auto) Road.
1869	The Cog Railway began its summer and fall passenger service up to the summit of Mount Washington.
1871	The U.S. Signal Service established a summit weather station.
1872–73	The second Summit House was constructed. The Boston & Maine Railroad and the Cog Railway financed the house in 1877. The daily newspaper *Among the Clouds* was first published here on the summit of Mount Washington. This was a two-and-a-half-story house.
1899	The first engine-powered vehicle ascended the mountain's Auto Road.
1915	The third Summit House was opened to the public.
1926	The famous musher Arthur T. Walden, a famed breeder of sled dogs, drove his team of huskies to the summit of Mount Washington and back in fifteen hours.
1932	The first Mount Washington Observatory was founded.
1932	Mrs. Florence Clark was the first woman to drive a team of five Eskimo sled dogs to the top of Mount Washington unassisted.
1934	The highest land wind velocity ever recorded (231 miles per hour) took place on the summit of Mount Washington.
1937	The first Mount Washington Observatory building constructed.
1938	A September hurricane blew on the summit of Mount Washington, ripping up twenty-four hundred feet of track of the Cog Railway and seriously damaging two structures at the base station.
1951	Cog Railway owner Colonel Henry Teague died and willed the railway and holdings to Dartmouth College.
1961	Arthur Teague became the new owner of the Cog Railway

1964	The State of New Hampshire purchased the summit property and buildings from Dartmouth College.
1971	The Mount Washington State Park was established at the summit.
1973	The Mount Washington Museum opened.
1975	The new Presidential Range–Dry River Wilderness was created by Congress.
1980	The Sherman Adams Summit Building, built by the State of New Hampshire, was opened to the public and became the year-round home of the Mount Washington Observatory and crew.
1993	The United States Forest Service completed the purchase of 857 acres at the eastern base of the mountain. This land was purchased from the Mount Washington Summit Road Company.
2004	Work was completed on replacing the lower Waumbet Switch and Siding.
2004	The Cog Railway began its first-time winter operations, taking skiers part way up the western side of Mount Washington.
2008	The Presby and Bedor families celebrated twenty-five years as owners of the Mount Washington Cog Railway.
2008	The first of four new biodiesel locomotives were christened by New Hampshire governor John Lynch.

Appendix B

Chronological List

of Locomotives

The following is a current list of Cog Railway locomotives. Abbreviations for builders are as follows:

CW = Campbell, Whittier & Co.
MLW = Manchester Locomotive Works
WA = Walter Aiken, Franklin, NH
CRS = Mt. Washington Cog Railway Shop

Date	Name	Type	Builder	Notes
1866	*Hero (Peppersass)	Steam	CW	The world's first cog locomotive. Retired in 1878.
1868	*George Stephenson	Steam	WA	Scrapped in 1878.
1870	*Atlas	Steam	WA	Replaced in 1875.
1870	*Cloud	Steam	WA	Replaced in 1876.
1874	Hercules	Steam	MLW	First locomotive built with a horizontal-type boiler.
1874	Kancamagnus	Steam	MLW	Originally built as first #6 Tip-Top. Rebuilt into second #6, named Great Gulf.

Date	Name	Type	Builder	Notes
1875	Ammonoosuc	Steam	MLW	#4 Atlas. Renumbered to #2, later named Ammonoosuc.
1875	*Atlas	Steam	WA	Damaged in fire in 1895 and scrapped.
1876	*Cloud	Steam	WA	Damaged in fire in 1895 and scrapped.
1878	*Eagle	Steam	MLW	Damaged by fire in 1895.
1878	*Tip-Top	Steam	MLW	Used cylinders of Great Gulf # 6.
1878	Great Gulf	Steam	MLW	Originally named Tip-Top.
1883	Falcon	Steam	MLW	Damaged by fire in 1895.
1883	Mt. Washington	Steam	MLW	Was the first # 7 Falcon, later renumbered and renamed Mt. Washington.
1883	Summit	Steam	MLW	Former #1 Mt. Desert, Green Mt. Cog Railway.
1883	Moosilauke	Steam	MLW	Originally #1, later became the third #4, named Summit. Renamed Chocorua. In 2008, it inherited #8.
1883	Agiocochook	Steam	MLW	Originally #2 in 1995. Renamed Agiocochook.
1892	Pilgrim	Steam	MLW	One of two engines with a Diamond smokestack.
1892	Tip-Top	Steam	MLW	Originally named Pilgrim, later renamed Tip-Top.
1908	Waumbek	Steam	Alco-MLW	First horizontal boiler. For a short time, this locomotive burned biodiesel. Later reconverted to coal.
1972	Kroflite	Steam	CRS	Boiler built by Munroe Boiler. Converted to burn oil and later named Colonel Teague.

DATE	NAME	TYPE	BUILDER	NOTES
1972	Colonel Teague	Steam	CRS	
2008	Wajo Babatassis	Diesel	CRS	First diesel- hydraulic locomotive.
2009	Algonquin	Diesel	CRS	Second diesel- hydraulic locomotive.
2009	Abenaki	Diesel	CRS	Third diesel-hydraulic locomotive.
2010	Agiocochook	Diesel	CRS	Fourth diesel- hydraulic locomotive.
	Col. Teague	Diesel	CRS	

*Locomotive with upright boilers only.

BIBLIOGRAPHY

Anderson, John, and Morse Sterns. *The Book of the White Mountains.* New York: Minton, Balch & Company, 1930.

Beals, Charles E. *Passaconaway in the White Mountains.* N.p.: Badger Publishers, 1916.

Belcher, Francis. "Trolly." *Appalachia* 31, no. 3 (1957).

Belknap, Jeremy. *History of New Hampshire.* Dover, NH: S.C. Stevens and Ela & Wadleigh, 1831.

Bisbee, Ernest E. *The White Mountain Scrapbook.* Lancaster, NH: Bisbee Press, 1946.

Boston, Concord & Montreal Railroad. *Summer Outings.* 1890s.

Boston & Maine Railroad. *Among the Mountains.* Boston, 1898.

———. *The White Mountains of New Hampshire.* Boston, 1902.

Browne, G. Waldo. *The Franconia Gateway.* Manchester, NH, 1920.

Burt, Frank H. *Among the Clouds.* Gorham, NH, 1888.

Chisholm's White Mountain Guidebook. N.p., 1880.

Cog Railway. *Mount Washington Railway Company.* Mount Washington, NH, 2010.

Concord & Montreal Railroad. *Summer Outings in the Granite State.* Boston, 1890.

Drake, Samuel A. *The Heart of the White Mountains.* Boston, 1882.

Harper's Weekly. "Into Cloudland by Car." August 21, 1869.

Heald, Bruce D. *Boston & Maine in the 19th Century.* Charleston, SC: Arcadia Publishing Co., 2000.

————. *Boston & Maine in the 20th Century.* Charleston, SC: Arcadia Publishing Co., 2001.

————. *Boston & Maine Trains and Service.* Charleston, SC Arcadia Publishing Co., 2005.

Joslin, Richard S. *Sylvester Marsh and the Cog Railway.* Tilton, NH: Sant Bani Press, 2000.

Kidder, Glen M. *Railway to the Moon.* Littleton, NH, 1969.

Kilborne, Frederick W. *Chronicles of the White Mountains.* Boston, 1916.

King, Thomas Starr. *The White Mountains.* Boston: Crosby and Nichols, 1864.

Lantos, Steve. *New Hampshire Handbook.* 1st ed. Chico, CA: Moon Publications, Inc., 1998.

Leavitt, Richard F. *Yesterday's New Hampshire.* Miami, FL: E.A. Seemann Publishing, Inc., 1974.

Little, William. *The White Mountains.* N.p.: James R. Osgood and Company, 1876.

McClintock, John N. *New Hampshire History.* Concord, NH, 1889.

Mount Washington Auto Road. "History." wikipedia.org/wiki/ MountWashingtonAuto Road.

Mount Washington Cog Railway. Brochure. 1966.

Mount Washington Observatory and Museum. Brochure. 2010.

Mount Washington Railway Company. *Historic Timeline.* N.d.

Mount Washington in Winter. Tour brochure. 1870–71.

National Register Information System. *National Register of Historic Places.* National Park Service, n.d.

New Hampshire Division of Parks & Recreation. *The Tip-Top House.* N.p., n.d.

New Hampshire Railroad Commission. *The New Hampshire Department of Transportation.* 1900.

Olsen, John. "The 1st Team to Summit of Mount Washington." *Appalachia* 18, no. 4 (June 1951).

Osgood's White Mountain Guide. N.p., 1884.

Pillsbury, Hobart. *New Hampshire History.* New York: Lewis Historical Publishing Company, 1929.

Poole, Earnest. *The Great White Hills of New Hampshire.* Garden City, NY: Doubleday, 1946.

"Preliminary Report of the Mt. Washington Cog Railway Accident—Issued by the Transportation Director W.E. Melvin of the New Hampshire Public Utilities Commission." *New Hampshire Sunday News,* September 24, 1967.

Roberts, Reverend Guy. *Old Peppersass.* 10th ed. Whitefield, NH, 1930.

Roberts, Reverend Guy, and Frank H. Burt. *Mount Washington: Its Past and Present.* 4th ed. Whitefield, NH, 1927.

Shorey, Guy L. "The Great Fire on Mount Washington." *Appalachia* 30 (June 1968).

Smith, Steve D., and Mike Dickerman. *Mount Washington: A Short Guide & History.* Littleton, NH: Bondcliff Books, 2007.

Spaulding, John H. *White Mountain Guide Historic Relics.* Littleton, NH: Bondcliff Books, 1998.

"Summit House." Catskillarchives.com.

Sweetzer, M.F. *Chisholm's White Mountain Echo.* Bethlehem, NH, 1879.

Teague, Ellen Crawford. *I Conquered My Mountain: The Autobiography of Ellen Crawford Teague.* Caanan, NH: Phoenix Publishing, 1982.

"The Tip Top House." New Hampshire.com

Waite, Otis, ed. *Eastman's White Mountains Guide.* Concord, NH: E.C. Eastman, 1895.

Wikipedia, s.v. "Mount Washington Cog Railway." http://en.wikipedia.org/wiki/Mount_Washington_Cog_Railway.

———. "Presidential Range." http://en.wikipedia.org/wiki/Presidential_Range.

Wood, Richard G. "Sylvester Marsh's Railroad." *Appalachia* 28, no. 2 (1950).

Workers of the Federal Writers Project, American Guide Series. *New Hampshire.* Boston: Houghton Mifflin Co., 1938.

.

INDEX

About the Author

Bruce Heald, adjunct faculty at Plymouth State University, History Department, and associate professor at Babes-Bolyai University, Cluj-Napoea, Romania, is also senior purser aboard the MS *Mount Washington* (forty-three years) and author of thirty-four books and numerous articles about the history and heritage of New England and the Lakes Region of New Hampshire. Dr. Heald is a graduate of Boston University, the University of Massachusetts at Lowell and Columbia Pacific University and holds a PhD in education. He is presently a fellow in the International Biography Association and the World Literary Academy in Cambridge, England. Dr. Heald is the recipient of the Gold Medal of Honor for literary achievement from the American Biographical Institute (1993). From 2005 to 2008, he was a state representative to the General Court of New Hampshire. Dr. Heald resides in Meredith, New Hampshire, with his family.